Blessen

In christ's Service

Jim Wick

THE GOSPEL
for the
WAYFARING

A Theology All Can Relate To

JIM WICK

WESTBOW
PRESS®
A DIVISION OF THOMAS NELSON
& ZONDERVAN

WestBow Press books may be ordered through booksellers or by contacting:

WestBow Press
A Division of Thomas Nelson & Zondervan
1663 Liberty Drive
Bloomington, IN 47403
www.westbowpress.com
844-714-3454

ISBN: 978-1-6642-3510-6 (sc)
ISBN: 978-1-6642-3511-3 (hc)
ISBN: 978-1-6642-3509-0 (e)

Library of Congress Control Number: 2021910291

Print information available on the last page.

WestBow Press rev. date: 6/28/2021

ACKNOWLEDGMENTS

As with most writers, I did not write in a vacuum and want to acknowledge those people that were intimately involved in getting this book to publication.

First is a godly wife who not only supported me but actively encouraged me along the way, especially when the going got tough. I began writing the book in late 2019 while still serving in the Philippines. Soon after getting started and abut fifty pages in, the COVID pandemic hit and halted the work until we were finally able to get back to the USA and settled in. And by then it was extremely difficult to get back to the project. However, my wife Grace, was a big encourager.

Another great help was my mother-in-law Kathleen O'Reilly who prodded me along and encouraged me to get back to writing when it was easier for me to claim to be "too busy". Thank you, Kathleen, you your insistence to keep going. She also was my main editor and did a great job.

And then there is Lonny Burke, a retired Bible College theology professor of many years who was willing to read the manuscript and give me some valuable insight.

And of course, God the Holy Spirit, who gave me the anointing and strength to record the insights He has taught me over my lifetime.

INTRODUCTION

I spent many years teaching at a Bible College and rubbing shoulders with people who prided themselves on their education and scholarly approach to studying the Bible. Now to be honest, I struggled with that approach somewhat but gave in to the temptation to approach the Bible with the scholarly mindset, at least in public, but continued to struggle on a personal level.

Most of the struggle was because of how God had conditioned me to study the Bible over the early part of my life. My parents raised me in the Church and taught me to read using the old King James version of the Bible. I grew up through my school years until high school, in church run schools and gained a deep love for God's Word. Even as a young adult, God allowed me to plant and pastor a small church in Montana and it was there that I developed the habit of studying the Bible on my knees with the Bible laying on the bed in front of me and I would prayerfully read and meditate on the Scriptures. Therefore, when I, in midlife decided to go back to school, I had to modify my approach to study. I first went to Bible College and upon graduation immediately went to Seminary and then immediately into the PhD program at Gonzaga University School of Education in Spokane, Washington. It was during my Seminary study at George Fox Evangelical Seminary that I was hired to teach at a small Bible School in 1994. Then in 1996 toward the end of my PhD studies, I was hired at a four-year Bible College and worked there until 2010.

Of course, it was during this time of formal training and teaching at the college level where I adopted the critical scholarly form of Bible study. The problem with this approach is that it forces one to depend on what others have said about some subject and is very difficult to approach the Scripture from a literal point of view. Now that is not always bad, because most people recognize that false teachings come from people who insist on adopting some personal philosophy and then proof-texting[1] to prove their point. And, when one is perfectly honest, that is the same approach that the "scholarly" method uses. In other words, when the scholar comes to some conclusion, the scholarly method insists that I cite sources that "prove" the point. And it is very easy to find sources that agree with almost any point I am trying to prove. It is very seldom that a scholar will quote some source that disagrees with them, so they quote 10 sources that say the same thing they are trying to prove and go away feeling good about themselves that they "proved" their point beyond any doubt. A problem with that approach is that I can take another point of view and find 10 other sources that agree with that point of view. So, at the Bible College where I worked, and this is true in most institutions of higher learning, faculty just adopt a "tolerance" for differing points of view. Now, I am not trying to say that this is all bad, because obviously some do stumble upon truth, and just as obvious, some people are more serious than others about finding and teaching truth. I am thankful for those years because they did force me to dig in and search more diligently for God's point of view.

Another hinderance to the scholarly method of Bible study in an academic setting is that the majority of institutions that teach Bible are private institutions. The Bible School where I taught was no exception. And because a private institution is not tax funded, it has to rely on student tuition to exist. Therefore, it is bound by certain cultural norms. To exist, most institutions will recruit students from a broad base of denominations and theological backgrounds. This forces administration to try as much as possible to cater to everyone, and to do that they must be more open to non-conforming ideas. For example, if a professor believed in the gifts of the Spirit but some of their students did not, then they could not openly teach that in the classroom for fear of offending a student

---

[1] Proof-texting is the practice of finding Scriptures that are taken out of context in an effort to prove the point you are trying to make

who did not believe it and the college loses the precious tuition. There is a certain bondage in not being able to teach the whole council of God. I have found it very liberating to be able to teach the whole of Scripture and not be censored for teaching certain controversial subjects.

Concluding my years of teaching at the Bible College, I went immediately as a missionary to the southern island of Mindanao, Philippines to develop a Bible school there. As my wife and I worked to develop a ministry there, God led us to the more remote and very poverty-stricken parts of the Philippines. As we began developing curriculum and teaching classes, it became evident almost immediately that the "American" scholarly approach to Bible study would not work in this culture. This is where my early experience and approach to Bible study began to resurface. I found that commentaries were not accepted at all because the education required to just read and understand what was being said was far beyond even the most educated. Of course, that is assuming that even American Bible college students had the ability to understand what was being taught. Consequently, we had to develop a curriculum that an uneducated people could understand. My original skeptical opinion of the scholarly approach to Bible study was verified, at least for anyone not involved in the scholarly circles of higher education, which, if one is honest, is the vast majority of people worldwide.

This people, although uneducated, and with virtually no availability to Bible study tools, still loved God with all their hearts and many were born again of the Spirit of God but simply could not understand scholarly language. Now I must insert here that not everyone we had as a student was uneducated. I was overwhelmed by the number of public-school teachers that enrolled in the Bible School. Nevertheless, what they needed was the Gospel in the language that they could understand and relate to in their context. The Philippines currently has about 90 active languages with two "official" languages; Filipino and English. The language that is spoken in the area that we minister in is Cebuano. While it is estimated that 15.8 million people speak the language[2], there is simply no Bible study tools available in the local language. Also, while in the larger cities where the average person has at least a high school education and can

---

[2] Cebuano Language - Structure, Writing & Alphabet - MustGo

speak the two national languages, they have access to some Bible study tools. However, out in the remote areas very few people have an education and therefore do not know the two national languages and have no access whatsoever to any Bible study tools. Cebuano does have several versions of the Bible in their language, but no commentaries, Bible dictionaries, concordance, etc. Therefore, what can be taught about the Bible must be taught in simple enough terms that they cannot misunderstand, as God clearly said was possible through Isaiah the prophet.

This revelation led me to a familiar verse in Isaiah's prophesy where he said that the Gospel was so simple that even "fools" (wayfaring men) could understand it.[3] I felt the Lord speak to me that His intention was that the Gospel should be presented in simple enough language that even an uneducated person could understand it. This challenged me to develop curriculum that would present the Bible and Christian theology in language simple enough that even my students in the remote mountain areas of the Southern Philippines could understand and grow into ministers in the Kingdom. As of this writing, we have graduated several hundred students and raised up four people who have become teachers in the Bible School bringing much fruit into the Kingdom.

Now, in case some might be offended by my description of uneducated people, I am not at all diminishing their value as people. There is nothing wrong with being uneducated according to the world's standards because most people recognize the fact that not all educated people are "smart", in fact the opposite is often the case. In fact, Paul pointed out this important fact to the Corinthian church.

> For you see your calling, brethren, that not many wise according to the flesh, not many mighty, not many noble, are called. But God has chosen the foolish things of the world to put to shame the wise, and God has chosen the weak things of the world to put to shame the things which are mighty; and the base things of the world and

---

[3] Isaiah 35:8 (KJV) "8 And an highway shall be there, and a way, and it shall be called The way of holiness; the unclean shall not pass over it; but it shall be for those: the wayfaring men, though fools, shall not err therein."

the things which are despised God has chosen, and the things which are not, to bring to nothing the things that are, that no flesh should glory in His presence. (1 Corinthians 1:26–29)

All I am saying is that the gospel message is so important that we need to present it in a manner where people cannot only understand it but cannot misunderstand it at whatever level of age or education the person might be. One of the valuable lessons I learned from my years of teaching at a Bible College was from a retired pastor who taught part time at the College. He had retired from pastoring a large church in Des Moines, Iowa and I invited him at least once a year to speak in a couple of my classes. He was a successful pastor and when asked what the "key to your success" was, he would respond with a story of his philosophy of teaching. He said that he always would personally identify a 12- or 13-year-old person in his congregation that he knew on a more personal level. He said that he would always prepare his sermons with that young person in mind because he knew that if he could preach in such a way that that young person could understand, then he could be confident that everyone in his congregation could learn. And that always stuck with me because it makes no difference one's economic or social status, God loves them the same and He died for them. If that is the case, then should not we, His ministers, be just as concerned that everyone God sends us to should hear to understanding?

So, that is the purpose of this book. I feel like there are many people around the world that just cannot relate to scholarly commentaries using the jargon of higher education when much of the world, including much of the church world, does not relate to the Bible on that higher scholarly level. There is a need for basic Bible study and theology to be studied on a level that even the "wayfaring" person can understand. Consequently, with the help and anointing of the Holy Spirit, I will attempt to explain the essence of Bible theology in basic language that the uneducated as well as the educated "shall not err therein" (Isaiah 35:8 KJV).

Please note that unless expressly stated, all Scripture quotations are taken from the NKJV of the Bible. ©1982, Thomas Nelson Publishers, Nashville, Atlanta.

1

IN THE BEGINNING

As with any discussion, one must start at the beginning; and in the case of theology, it is absolutely essential to begin there. Since the Bible begins with the words, "In the beginning God created the heavens and the earth" (Genesis 1:1), that is where I will begin also.

I intend to spend more time on this part of the Bible because I have become convinced, after many years of preaching, teaching and interacting with people, that without a clear understanding of what happened in the very beginning, one cannot understand much that is written in the Bible either. The fact of the matter is that the events in the beginning necessarily dictate what takes place in the rest of the Book, as well as dictating how we understand and interpret those events. Consequently, it is essential to have a clear understanding of these events. In fact, I believe that one could rightly argue that it is from a misunderstanding of what happened in the beginning that has led to most controversies in the church as well as being the source of most false doctrines.

Allow me to give you one clear example of what I mean. Jesus had been teaching for some time and had created some followers as well as many skeptics. But one highly educated man who we would probably refer to as a scholar today, although somewhat of a skeptic, recognized that Jesus was no ordinary man and desired to know more about Him and His teaching. As a respected Jewish leader this man, Nicodemus, was afraid to approach Jesus during the day in case a colleague should see him, thus he came to Jesus under cover of night. Now we need to clearly understand that this man was highly educated in the Scriptures, was a respected teacher in Jerusalem, therefore he should have had a deeper understanding of the Scriptures than the ordinary person on the street. In fact, Jesus even questioned him concerning his lack of understanding even though he was highly trained in the Scriptures – "Jesus answered and said to him, "Are you the teacher of Israel, and do not know these things?" (John 3:10).

It should be clear that the reason Nicodemus did not understand Jesus's words is because of a fundamental lack of understanding of what happened in the very beginning. If he had understood what happened in the beginning, he would have understood what Jesus was referring to when "Jesus answered and said to him, 'Most assuredly, I say to you, unless one is born again, he cannot see the kingdom of God'" (John 3:3). So, lest we make the same mistake and build our theology on a misunderstanding of Scripture as Nicodemus did, we need to return to the beginning and look for what he missed that caused him to misunderstand Jesus's teaching.

I must first lay down some ground rules for this discussion because there are some basic facts that we need to understand in order to follow the reasoning that leads to the truth. After spending many years in higher education, I have come to the conclusion that many Bible scholars study the Bible to death and when it is studied to death, as with any dead thing, it has no life left in it. I am not anti-intellectual and have devoted my life to higher education. But the fact of the matter is that too many scholars forget Jesus' foundational council to Nicodemus – "Jesus answered and said to him, "Most assuredly, I say to you, unless one is born again, he cannot see the kingdom of God" (John 3:3). As you continue reading understand that he said that one must be born again of the "Spirit", which, of course, meaning the Holy Spirit. So, he could not understand, not because he was uneducated and did not apply the correct hermeneutic principle[4], but Jesus meant that he lacked the Holy Spirit. Consequently, all popular Bible study methods are insufficient for understanding the Scriptures. But it must be by the Spirit who inspired the Scriptures in the

---

[4] the study of the general principles of biblical interpretation

first place who alone understands Scripture and, therefore, is the only One qualified to interpret what is written in Scripture. It is clear that while knowing and using some consistent Bible study methods is valid and important, what is more important is being filled with the Spirit of God and relying on Him to guide you into all understanding.

I am not advocating that just because a person claims to be "born again" does not automatically guarantee that they can rightly interpret and understand Scripture. If that were the case, we would have no need for Bible College education to prepare men and women for ministry. What I am saying is that one must begin with being filled with, or as many people say today, be born again or baptized in the Spirit of God as a foundation for their Bible study education. Jesus was very specific with Nicodemus that a person cannot understand or enter the Kingdom of God without it. On the other hand, Paul was clear also when he admonished Timothy "(b)e diligent to present yourself approved to God, a worker who does not need to be ashamed, rightly dividing the word of truth" (2 Timothy 2:15). Therefore, we learn two important things about Bible study here. First, one must be diligent. Some translations use the word "study to show yourself approved", which is a good interpretation of the original word. Where Paul said to be diligent and then used the word "worker", the implication is that to rightly divide the word of truth, one must diligently study the Scripture and allow the Holy Spirit to assist you in putting it all together. When I taught Bible Study classes at the Bible School in the Philippines, the very first class I would bring in a jigsaw puzzle and have the class put it together. This exercise served as a good example of what it took to rightly divide and understand the written word.

Just like a jigsaw puzzle, the Scripture comes to us in a thousand pieces, and God has given us the chore of putting it together so that we can see the whole picture. I believe that this is what Solomon meant when he penned this proverb. "It is the glory of God to conceal a matter, (b)ut the glory of kings is to search out a matter" (Proverbs 25:2). Far too often, scholars or preachers force a piece to fit where it does not belong, and the result is a distorted picture. I suspect that most readers will have at one time or another put together a puzzle and know what it looks like when you force a piece of the puzzle where it does not belong. We are given the solemn charge to work hard to ensure that each piece (verse) fits perfectly together (doctrine) so that when we present the picture to the lost and the disciples, it is a clear, full, accurate picture of God's intended purpose. My prayer for this book is that I might spur each reader on to be that diligent worker who will only settle for the pure undefiled word of God.

There is another principle that is important if one is to properly understand the Old Testament Scriptures. Listen to the Apostle Paul explain this important truth:

> However, we speak wisdom among those who are mature, yet not the wisdom of this age, nor of the rulers of this age, who are coming to nothing. But we speak the wisdom of God in a mystery, the hidden wisdom which God ordained before the ages for our glory, which none of the rulers of this age knew; for had they known, they would not have crucified the Lord of glory.
>
> But as it is written: "Eye has not seen, nor ear heard, nor have entered into the heart of man the things which God has prepared for those who love Him."
>
> But God has revealed them to us through His Spirit. For the Spirit searches all things, yes, the deep things of God. For what man knows the things of a man except the spirit of the man which is in him? Even so no one knows the things of God except the Spirit of God. Now we have received, not the spirit of the world, but the Spirit who is from God, that we might know the things that have been freely given to us by God. (1 Corinthians 2:6–12)

Notice this important point from verse 7, "But we speak the wisdom of God in a mystery, the hidden wisdom which God ordained before the ages for our glory". Why, we must ask, does God have "hidden" wisdom? The answer is found in the next verse: "which none of the rulers of this age knew; for had they known, they would not have crucified the Lord of glory." For that reason, we need to clearly understand that God had to hide some of His actions and their subsequent plans and revelations, because His arch enemy, Satan, was closely watching and listening. If God had clearly and openly declared all of His plan, Satan would have tried to hinder God's plan and would not have crucified Jesus, which of course, was the foundation of God's plan. This then should make us also understand that there was more to the temptation with Eve and Adam than merely a bite of fresh fruit from the forbidden tree. We will return to this subject later, but for now know that because there are some essential truths of God's plan hidden in the Old Testament Scriptures, we need to have the help of the New Testament revelation as well as the anointing of the indwelling Holy Spirit of God to give us understanding of these hidden truths. Paul also tells us that although there were hidden things in the Old Testament, they are revealed to us in the New Testament by the Spirit of God. "But God has revealed them to us through His Spirit. For the Spirit searches all things, yes, the deep things of God" (1 Corinthians 2:10).

The truth is, of course, is that if God had hidden something from the Old Testament saints, then it would of necessity be hidden to one studying the Old Testament today. I am convinced that many incomplete theologies have been developed by doing word studies strictly from the Old Testament. Again, if God hid something from them, then they are hidden, and we will not find them by studying the use of some Hebrew or Greek word or phrase. Jesus was so clear and specific in his conversation with Nicodemus, "I tell you the truth, no one can see the kingdom of God unless he is born again" (John 3:3b). So, I am convinced that to come to an accurate theology, one must, first of all be born again of the Spirit of God, and second, study the Old Testament and New Testament together. The Old Testament must be understood with New Testament understanding given by the Holy Spirit.

I feel compelled to add a short explanation here concerning my criticism of some Bible scholars. I had a good friend who taught Bible theology at a Bible college for many years who, when he read a draft of this chapter, made the comment that "your treatment of Bible scholars seems a little harsh!" And to be honest, I meant it to be because Jesus and Paul both used rather harsh words for the Pharisees, who were the Bible scholars of their day. Nevertheless, I need to admit that I know a number of Bible scholars personally and know them to be godly men and women who love Jesus with all their heart and desire to teach truth. My problem is not with them. I felt like I had to over-emphasize the point in order to make the important point that no matter how well one knows the Scripture, without the anointing of the Spirit of God, it is going to be incomplete and shallow.

With that understanding, we must turn briefly to the New Testament to get a picture of God's plan. Both the Apostles John and Peter use the phrase "born again" to describe the entrance into the Kingdom of God. Listen to John and Peter talk about this experience: "Jesus answered and said to him, 'Most assuredly, I say to you, unless one is born again, he cannot see the kingdom of God..... Do not marvel that I said to you, 'You must be born again'" (John 3:3 & 7). And Peter then speaks of the effects of this experience: "having been born again, not of corruptible seed but incorruptible, through the word of God which lives and abides forever" (1 Peter 1:23). It is also important to notice Peter's words, "which lives and abides forever". In other words, when we are born again of the Spirit of God, we can count on it being from God, and it is very much alive which means that we can depend on Him to always be there when we need Him.

All right, you might argue, what does that have to do with the beginning? Good question. If one must be "born again" then logically that must mean that there was a first time you were born, and something happened so that now it must be done again. Or, as some would argue, as Nicodemus ask Jesus, does it mean that one has to be born a second time? And, regardless of how you phrase the question, indeed, that is the case. We must now return to the beginning and walk our way through the events, using New Testament revelation to make sense of what happened and why. Remember that we must depend on the Holy Spirit for understanding and expect that there is something hidden that should be revealed in the New Testament.

In Genesis chapter one, we get the essence of God's plan and purpose for His human creation. Most of us are familiar with the record found there.

> Then God said, "Let Us make man in Our image,
> according to Our likeness; let them have dominion over
> the fish of the sea, over the birds of the air, and over the
> cattle, over all the earth and over every creeping thing
> that creeps on the earth." So God created man in His
> own image; in the image of God He created him; male
> and female He created them. Then God blessed them,
> and God said to them, "Be fruitful and multiply; fill the
> earth and subdue it; have dominion over the fish of the
> sea, over the birds of the air, and over every living thing
> that moves on the earth (Genesis 1:26–28).

Now as we begin to unpack this event, we must first understand a very important truth so we don't come to a wrong conclusion. I have read many commentaries by acclaimed scholars who are fluent in the original biblical languages who have come to the conclusion that the words "spirit" and "soul" are used interchangeably and therefore are referring to the same thing. However, keep in mind that God's ultimate goal was concealed and therefore not visible in the Old Testament. So, it doesn't take a brain surgeon to conclude that if something is hidden, it therefore cannot be seen. Consequently, a word study of only Old Testament words, no matter how well done, will not reveal ultimate spiritual truth without New Testament revelation anointed by the Holy Spirit of God.

Now, with these things clearly in mind we need to carefully unpack this beginning revelation of God's purpose and activity in creation. First, it would seem, it would be wise to clearly understand what God "is", since He chose to make mankind in "His image". The Bible speaks in several places of God's substance, but never clearer than in Jesus's conversation with the woman at the well in John 4:24 where Jesus declared that "God is Spirit, and those who worship Him must worship in spirit and truth". So obviously, the only logical conclusion one can come to is that God created a human spirit if it was truly in His "image". The Bible is clear that God is not a man of flesh, but His substance is Spirit. Now here it is important to make a quick note of an essential truth that is often missed. We know that God is Spirit and is uncreated. That is, He has always existed and will always exist and is the Creator of all things. Consequently, God is NOT a created Spirit, He is uncreated. Nevertheless, He did create a spirit that was in His image for the human beings He was creating. So, while the Spirit that He created for the human race was in His image, it was not divine in the sense that it was not an eternal spirit. This essential truth is important in both understanding what happened in the garden in Genesis and what happens in the "born again" experience that is revealed in the New Testament. So, it is important from this point to follow closely the sequence of events involved in the creation of mankind.[5]

We see first that God began with a "spirit" that was created in God's image and according to His likeness. Some have tried to somehow link God's "image" to the human psyche[6] or link it in some other way to the physical body. However, that point of view simply does not stand up to the revelation in the rest of Scripture. But as we continue reading we find that there was more to the process. Note especially Genesis chapter 2; "And the Lord God formed man of the dust of the ground and breathed into his nostrils the breath of life; and man became a living being" (Genesis 2:7). Now closely follow the remaining sequence of God's creation of mankind. As we read carefully, we discover that creation of humans was a three-step process. Although it must be understood that only one part was created, while the other two parts simply used material that was already in existence. First of course, as we have already seen is the human spirit, but now we see that God made the body from the dust of the earth which, of course already existed. Imagine if you will, God opening a package of Playdough and forming what looks like a human body. Of course, if you have ever witnessed a dead body you will get an image of what this might have looked like. A hunk of clay that looks like a human, but has no animation or personality attached with it. But then the third step is

---

[5] I have overused the words "create" and "created on purpose to emphasize the difference between "to create" and "to form" or "to make". To create is to cause something that does not already exist to appear (Romans 4:17), and "to form" refers to something that was made or formed from something that already existed (created).

[6] The human "psyche" is another term for the human "soul", that part of mankind that contains the mind, the will, and the emotions. Psyche is the scientific term used in today's understanding.

important to notice now. Look at the last part of verse 7; "and breathed into his nostrils the breath of life; and man became a living being." Did you note the three specific steps of God's creation of the human being? The first step was creation of the male and female spirit, then there was the formation of a body, and last of all the breath of life, which we must note used the air that was already in existence. And now, finally, this human creation was a fully formed and functioning human being. Many translations use the word soul, in place of the word being, but the facts remain the same. The spirit is what connects this human being to God's Image and gives them "dominion", while the body is the shell where this created spirit lives and then finally, when God gives it breath live it became a fully functioning human with soul. We can conclude then that the soul is that part which gives us personality, usually described as the mind, will, and emotion of the human person. It is obvious that when the "breath" goes out of a person, we use the term "died" because they no longer have animation, will, or emotion which is usually described as the personality of the person.

I trust you picked up on the important theological point that God created humans as a three part being; first He created the spirit, then he formed the body and last, he instilled the soul or life. Pay close attention to the sequence because if we lose sight of the sequence and what precisely happened in each step in the sequence we will be led into error, or at the least, a gross misunderstanding of essential truth. To summarize then, the spirit was created (in God's image), the body was formed, that is it was not created but formed out of what was already there, and the breath of life was not created either, but was simply the air that was already present. This point will be important in understanding the current human condition.

God gave this newly created human several duties. First, "God blessed them, and God said to them, 'Be fruitful and multiply; fill the earth and subdue it; have dominion over the fish of the sea, over the birds of the air, and over every living thing that moves on the earth'" (Genesis 1:28). And then of course, God made just one demand on this newly created, formed couple:

Then the Lord God took the man and put him in the garden of Eden to tend and keep it. And the Lord God commanded the man, saying, "Of every tree of the garden you may freely eat; but of the tree of the knowledge of good and evil you shall not eat, for in the day that you eat of it you shall surely die. (Genesis 2:15–17)

THE NEED TO BE BORN AGAIN

The scene is now set, and the drama about to unfold. Consequently, it is imperative that we pay close attention to what happened. Just like it was imperative to closely follow the sequence of events to arrive at a correct view of creation, so it is imperative that we pay close attention to the sequence of events to correctly understand what happened at what is usually referred to as "the fall". The lack of focus and confusion concerning what events are at the heart of much misunderstanding for far too many people, including most "educated" scholars who, as Nicodemus did, fail to grasp the truth. Please bear with me as we take a very slow but deliberate walk through the next series of events to discover what is there.

I feel it necessary to briefly stop and summarize what we have discovered to this point before moving on to a look at God's next steps. God said very clearly that Adam and Eve were not to eat of the fruit of this one tree, the tree of the knowledge of good and evil. Why should they not eat of it? Simple. ". . . for in the day that you eat of it you shall surely die!" (Genesis 2:17). Notice that God said that in "the day" that they chose to eat of the fruit from this tree, they would die. He did NOT say that they would begin to die, or that the process of death would begin. No! God expressly said that they would die in the very day that they ate. So, we cannot rightly put some other meaning to it and be correct. Subsequently, let's look at the story with this truth clearly in mind.

Notice what happened next. God completed creation and eventually formed Eve as a companion for Adam and a recipient of the female spirit that God had previously created in the Image of God. She was formed from the rib of Adam and the dust of the ground, and then just as with

Adam, God breathed into her the breath of life and she as well was a complete person, spirit, body, and soul/personality.

> Now the serpent was more cunning than any beast of the field which the Lord God had made. And he said to the woman, "Has God indeed said, 'You shall not eat of every tree of the garden'?"
>
> And the woman said to the serpent, "We may eat the fruit of the trees of the garden; but of the fruit of the tree which is in the midst of the garden, God has said, 'You shall not eat it, nor shall you touch it, lest you die.'"
>
> Then the serpent said to the woman, "You will not surely die. For God knows that in the day you eat of it your eyes will be opened, and you will be like God, knowing good and evil."
>
> So when the woman saw that the tree was good for food, that it was pleasant to the eyes, and a tree desirable to make one wise, she took of its fruit and ate. She also gave to her husband with her, and he ate (Genesis 3:1–7).

As we consider this account, remember the New Testament revelation that there were some events pertaining to God's plan of salvation that He kept secret, so it should become obvious that we must consult the New Testament revelation to properly understand what took place here. You should as well recognize similar language between the events in Genesis pertaining to Adam and Eve's "fall" and Jesus's conversation with Nicodemus. It seems that it was a real tree with real fruit of some kind. In the Western church, most people picture an apple as the fruit that they ate, but after living in the Philippines for many years surrounded with an abundance of tropical fruits, I can just imagine a variety of sweet juicy tropical fruit of some kind; like a mango, or maybe a papaya!

Notice carefully what the immediate consequences were when Eve

11

and Adam took their first bite of this forbidden fruit. "Then the eyes of both of them were opened, and they knew that they were naked; and they sewed fig leaves together and made themselves coverings" (Genesis 3:7). Think very carefully through this revelation keeping clearly in mind what we already know. Remember that they were created a three part being, spirit, body and soul. So, as we consider the circumstances, we must realize that their body did not die, for they still had their bodies, they were just now aware for the first time that they were naked. We know that they still had their soul which is where the mind, will and emotions dwell, because they could now be embarrassed when they realized that they were naked. We have to conclude, therefore, that it was not their soul that died because they could still feel shame. We read in Genesis 3:8 that "... And they heard the sound of the Lord God walking in the garden in the cool of the day, and Adam and his wife hid themselves from the presence of the Lord God among the trees of the garden." Therefore, we are forced to conclude that they still had their body and they still possessed breath life that is their soul. So, what died? It seems obvious that they lost their sense of holiness or innocence which is only available with God's presence, which when we consider Jesus's words to Nicodemus is only available to humans through the Spirit of God. Remember Jesus's word in John 3:2 "Jesus answered and said to him, "Most assuredly, I say to you, unless one is born again, he cannot see the kingdom of God."

You should be asking along with Nicodemus, "why does one have to be born again?" And, when we understand all the facts revealed to us by the historical account in Genesis and Jesus spiritual account revealed in His answer with Nicodemus, the answer should be just as obvious. When God said that "in the day" that they ate of the forbidden fruit they would die, that in fact, they did die, God is speaking of the spirit part of them. Not their body, not their soul, but their spirit died. Now with this revelation, it becomes clear why Jesus told Nicodemus that he must be born again. From the time that Adam and Eve's spirit died, mankind became a body and soul, but without a spirit. That is why they could not "see" God or were not able to obey Him; they lacked the one essential part that would allow them to communicate with God, a spirit. No wonder Jesus told Nicodemus that without the spirit they could not "see" and could not "enter" the Kingdom of God. Without the spirit mankind does not even have the equipment with which to "see" God. Now, some will point to Romans chapter 1 and argue that they do. But Paul's point in Romans is not concerning being born again but it is grace. True, they are related, and we will talk at some length later in this book about grace, but here we have to understand that we need to be born again of the spirit before we can even begin to understand grace or salvation, or for that matter any other matter discussed in all of Scripture.

THE TWO BIRTHS EXPLAINED

Here we must pause for a moment and go back and look at Jesus's conversation with Nicodemus in its entirety. Note carefully that to understand Jesus's point we must consider the full conversation which is recorded for us in John's gospel. Here Jesus explains not only the necessity of being born again, but also the means of being reborn as well as the heart attitude and purpose of God in providing a way for mankind to be reborn.

> There was a man of the Pharisees named Nicodemus, a ruler of the Jews. This man came to Jesus by night and said to Him, "Rabbi, we know that You are a teacher come from God; for no one can do these signs that You do unless God is with him."

> Jesus answered and said to him, "Most assuredly, I say to you, unless one is born again, he cannot see the kingdom of God."

> Nicodemus said to Him, "How can a man be born when he is old? Can he enter a second time into his mother's womb and be born?"

> Jesus answered, "Most assuredly, I say to you, unless one is born of water and the Spirit, he cannot enter the kingdom of God. That which is born of the flesh is flesh,

and that which is born of the Spirit is spirit. Do not marvel that I said to you, 'You must be born again.' The wind blows where it wishes, and you hear the sound of it, but cannot tell where it comes from and where it goes. So is everyone who is born of the Spirit."

Nicodemus answered and said to Him, "How can these things be?"

Jesus answered and said to him, "Are you the teacher of Israel, and do not know these things? Most assuredly, I say to you, We speak what We know and testify what We have seen, and you do not receive Our witness. If I have told you earthly things and you do not believe, how will you believe if I tell you heavenly things? No one has ascended to heaven but He who came down from heaven, that is, the Son of Man who is in heaven. And as Moses lifted up the serpent in the wilderness, even so must the Son of Man be lifted up, that whoever believes in Him should not perish but have eternal life. For God so loved the world that He gave His only begotten Son, that whoever believes in Him should not perish but have everlasting life. For God did not send His Son into the world to condemn the world, but that the world through Him might be saved.

"He who believes in Him is not condemned; but he who does not believe is condemned already, because he has not believed in the name of the only begotten Son of God. And this is the condemnation, that the light has come into the world, and men loved darkness rather than light, because their deeds were evil. For everyone practicing evil hates the light and does not come to the light, lest his deeds should be exposed. But he who does

the truth comes to the light, that his deeds may be clearly
seen, that they have been done in God" (John 3:1–21).

Upon reading this conversation between Jesus and Nicodemus, we
need to pay special attention to where the conversation begins and where
it ends because we don't dare try to understand Jesus's teaching with
only part of the conversation in view. Of course, one of the foundational
principals of Bible study is to always read the account in its full context.
Verse one and the first part of verse two set the stage while the second
half of verse two through verse 21 record the conversation.

One of the excessively misunderstood statements is found in verse
five. "Jesus answered, 'Most assuredly, I say to you, unless one is born of
water and the Spirit, he cannot enter the kingdom of God.'"

Many people argue that Jesus is saying that a person must be baptized
in water and the Spirit. But this is a dangerous misinterpretation of what
Jesus said. Remember again that one of the basic principles of Bible
interpretation says that one must understand everything in the context
of which it was written. Consequently, when one reads it in context, it
becomes clear that Jesus is not talking about water baptism but rather
He is talking about birth. And there is a vast difference between birth
and baptism. Although, I acknowledge that many in the modern church
do refer to the born-again experience as the baptism in the Spirit. And
while this might be appropriate language, it can be misleading if not
properly understood. For this reason, we cannot read "baptism" into
this verse without doing great disservice to the verse, not to mention our
theology. Most of us surely understand that a human baby is housed in
an amniotic sac of water in the mother's womb. In fact, one of the first
signs that a baby is ready to be born is when the mother's "water" breaks.
A term that has been used and understood for thousands of years. Jesus
is simply saying that a person, who is to take part in the eternal Kingdom
of God must be born of water, that is born in the natural way into this
world as a human, created in God's image, but with a full one third of his
or her being missing. Then that person must be born again of the Spirit of
God and become a fully functioning human in God's image once again.
However, now with the Spirit of God Himself residing within ready to

take on the responsibility of having dominion over God's creation just like He commanded the first human couple to do thousands of years ago.

Now it is impossible to fully understand the consequences of Eve and Adam's sin apart from a clear comprehension of what the exchange between Eve and the serpent involved. And it is equally impossible to understand the present human condition without a clear understanding of the consequences of their sin. I must speculate a bit here because the historical account in Scripture is not extremely clear. I will take the account that is clear and try to fill in the gaps to help us understand what the motive was both on Eve's part and on the serpent's (the Devil's) part. God created all the heavenly host including the angels and gave them their charge and duties. The three arch angels seem to have been Lucifer, Michael and Gabriel, each given charge over a third of the angels that God created; each had their specific charge and duties. Lucifer seems to have been such a beautiful and talented creature that he became lifted up with pride and challenged God for the position of God and the dominion in heaven. God, of course, expelled him from his position and as Jesus later testified "I saw Satan fall like lightning from heaven" (Luke 10:18–19). Well, it seems that this did not stop Lucifer's quest for dominion that he so lusted after. So, when God created the world and made the decision to give the newly created humans dominion over God's creation, this made Lucifer, better known as Satan, so jealous that he set his heart on somehow stealing this dominion for himself.

Now fast forward to the Garden of Eden where Satan (in the form of a serpent) found Eve and began a conversation in which he questioned the goodness and wisdom of God in forbidding them from eating from this one tree. It appears unmistakable that the issue was not some piece of fruit but the very dominion that God had bestowed on this human couple. Satan thought that it was his due and he was extremely jealous of this human couple and uncontrollably angry at God for not giving the dominion of the earth to him. Consequently, he set about to deceive God's newly created couple into partaking of the forbidden fruit. Satan must have known the characteristic of God that "... the gifts and the calling of God are irrevocable" (Romans 11:29). Therefore, he was confident that once he was able to get Adam and Eve to revoke their right to God's dominion that God would honor His word and it would indeed be his. You see, true dominion is a spiritual power and does not come to or by way of frail flesh and blood. So, once he could get them to disobey and partake of the forbidden fruit, their spirit, created in the image of God, would die which in turn would end their dominion and Satan would simply take legal possession of it and because God always keeps His word, therefore, God would not come and take it away from him by force. When God gives you something, because He will not renege on it, you are free to do whatever you please with it. This truth is not explained any better than in Psalm 15:4,

But he honors those who fear the Lord;

He who swears to his own hurt and does not change;

True, you are responsible for what you do with it, but when God gives you anything, it is yours and you can keep it and use it, keep it but put in in your closet and forget that you even have it, or you can give it away to someone else. How many of us have ever been given a gift, say for a birthday or for Christmas and because we did not want it, we simply gave it away to someone else. After all, it was yours and you could do whatever you pleased with it. The same is true of the gifts from God. I will return to a more in-depth discussion of this topic when I get to the gifts of the Spirit in a later chapter.

Eve and Adam did succumb to the temptation presented by the serpent/Satan and did indeed transfer their God given dominion to Satan. The Apostle Paul revealed another major truth regarding the character of God in his letter to the Romans; "And we know that all things work together for good to those who love God, to those who are the called according to His purpose" (Romans 8:28). Let me again remind you that God had to keep His ultimate purpose deeply hidden because it was essential that Satan not know the details of how God was going to legally regain the stolen dominion and return it to mankind once again (1 Corinthians 2:8). Remember that God is not only a God of love, He is also a God of justice. It is like two sides of a coin, you can't have one side without the other. Justice means that you treat everyone the same, you are no respecter of persons and when you swear to something, you keep your word even to your own detriment. Listen again to the Psalmist speaking of a godly person as one who when "He who swears to his own hurt and does not change;" (Psalm 15:4). In other words, when you make a promise or give your word on something, you keep your word, even when things do not turn out like you wanted them to. And this was certainly the case here. God created humankind with the intention that they would exercise dominion over God's creation and take good care of it. When Adam and Eve chose to disobey and turn over legal control of creation to Satan, because God is a just God, He was deeply disappointed, but He did not just step in and take that dominion back, although I think one could convincingly argue that He certainly could have had He chosen to. Nevertheless, He had given it to Adam and Eve, and they consequently had the legal right to do whatever they wanted with it. There were predetermined consequences for their behavior, nevertheless, God limited Himself to legally regaining dominion and the only way to do that was to pay the legal penalty for Adam's sin, and gain it back legally and rightfully. God already had plans on doing exactly that, but, again, He had to keep it a closely guarded secret lest Satan discover the plan and thwart it.

To ensure that we all understand this transfer of dominion and its consequences, we need to look at several New Testament Scriptures. I want to begin with somewhat of a controversial verse to make the point because we find Satan himself making the claim to Jesus during Jesus' 40 days of fasting and trials in the wilderness.

> Then the devil, taking Him up on a high mountain, showed Him all the kingdoms of the world in a moment of time. And the devil said to Him, "All this authority I will give You, and their glory; for this has been delivered to me, and I give it to whomever I wish. Therefore, if You will worship before me, all will be Yours (Luke 4:5–7).

Notice if you will that the devil offered to give Jesus dominion over all creation. Why? "for it has been delivered to me, and I give it to whomever I wish". God gave it to Adam and Eve and future generations that would be born from them. However, notice what happened – they give it away to the serpent/devil! Now, I realize that some will respond; "Well, the devil is a liar and the father of lies (John 8:44), so how are we to believe him?" Good question! But Jesus did not argue with him one bit and I think one could successfully argue that on such an important issue, if Satan had been wrong, Jesus would have mentioned it.

Nevertheless, God has not left us with only the devil's word for it. Notice these other Scriptures referring to Satan or the devil as having dominion and as we search even deeper, we find that one of the reasons Jesus died and conquered death for us is so that He could regain that dominion that was given away. Notice that the Apostle Paul refers to Satan as "the god of this age" (2 Corinthians 4:4).

> "But even if our gospel is veiled, it is veiled to those who are perishing, whose minds the god of this age has blinded, who do not believe, lest the light of the gospel of the glory of Christ, who is the image of God, should shine on them" (2 Corinthians 4:3–4).

And then listen to the beloved Apostle John in his first letter: "We know that we are of God, and the whole world lies under the sway of the wicked one" (1 John 5:19). And we cannot forget most authors of the New Testament, recognizing who had dominion over God's creation, spoke freely of one of the results of Christ's accomplishments on the cross. I will elaborate more fully on this subject of dominion later, but for now listen to Peter identify the One who has dominion now:

> "If anyone speaks, let him speak as the oracles of God. If anyone ministers, let him do it as with the ability which God supplies, that in all things God may be glorified through Jesus Christ, to whom belong the **glory and the dominion forever** and ever. Amen" (1 Peter 4:11 Emphasis added).

Therefore, it should be clear that when Jesus Christ defeated the devil at Calvary, he legally regained the dominion that Adam and Eve lost. It should be clear by now that it is only as you and I abide in Christ, that we too regain dominion over God's creation once again.

Now, lest we give the devil too much credit, we need to see the result of that "secret" mission that was so important that God had to keep it hidden until He could complete His purpose for mankind. Let's quickly recap where we are at in our discussion. God created humankind in His image which was spirit and put them in charge (gave them dominion) of His creation with conditions. Those conditions were that they had to obey Him explicitly. When they disobeyed, their spirit immediately died and now they were only body and soul, or what Paul and James would later refer to as fleshly or carnal (see Romans 7:14 and James 2:26). That is without spirit. God, determined to redeem mankind and restore them back to what He originally intended, put a secret plan into action which culminated in the redemptive work of His only begotten Son, who we know as Jesus the Christ. Once Jesus, the long-promised Messiah was here, lived, died and rose from the dead, God could now reveal that long hidden secret to His people who the Scriptures reveal are only those who believe and are "born again." The issue that caused all this deception and forced God to carry out His secret mission was, as we have clearly seen was dominion over His creation. That is, who was going to be the god of this world that the only true God created. The winner, or so it seemed on the surface, was Lucifer/Satan. But now let's look in Scripture and see what the result of the Messiah's coming truly was. Notice first of all what John says; "He who sins is of the devil, for the devil has sinned from the beginning. **For this purpose**, the Son of God was manifested, that He might **destroy the works of the devil**" (1 John 3:8–9 Emphasis added).

And what are the works of the devil that Jesus destroyed? It is apparent that his works are many but the most obvious and tragic is death. While the immediate consequence was spiritual death, the humans now found themselves with no spirit and therefore, the bond with God was broken, and physical death resulted both for mankind and for all of creation. Notice how Paul explains this dilemma in Romans 8:18–23:

> For I consider that the sufferings of this present time
> are not worthy to be compared with the glory which

shall be revealed in us. For the earnest expectation of the **creation eagerly waits** for the revealing of the sons of God. For the **creation was subjected to futility**, not willingly, but because of Him who subjected it in hope; because the creation itself also will be delivered from the bondage of corruption into the glorious liberty of the children of God. For we know that the whole creation groans and labors with birth pangs together until now (Emphasis added).

Nevertheless, the most tragic work of the devil, death will also eventually be defeated as well. "The last enemy that will be destroyed is death" (1 Corinthians 15:26).

While we have established that the serpent/Satan was able to successfully gain legal dominion over God's creation, we need as well to understand that today he does not necessarily have to have dominion over everything. Remember that Jesus came to destroy the works of the devil and while he remains alive and active, he has no real power over God's people, nor does he have any weapons other than lies to fight against God's people. Listen to Paul teach this truth; "Having disarmed principalities and powers, He made a public spectacle of them, triumphing over them in it" (Colossians 2:15). So now I trust you are asking, "If Jesus destroyed the works of the devil, which was exercising dominion over God's creation, then who has dominion over God's creation now?" Well, we need to think carefully through the revelation of Scripture carefully because there is not a single Scripture that spells it all out clearly. But it becomes very clear when we follow Paul's advice to Timothy and rightly divide the word of truth (2 Timothy 2:15).

The following Scriptures, when put together will show who has legal dominion over creation today. Notice first that "For he has rescued us from the **dominion** of darkness and brought us into the kingdom of the Son he loves, in whom we have redemption, the forgiveness of sins"

(Colossians 1:13-14 NIV[7] emphasis added). And then the Apostle Paul in his letter to the Ephesians had this rather lengthy explanation:

> "that the God of our Lord Jesus Christ, the Father of glory, may give to you the spirit of wisdom and revelation in the knowledge of Him, the eyes of your understanding being enlightened; that you may know what is the hope of His calling, what are the riches of the glory of His inheritance in the saints, and what is the exceeding greatness of His power toward us who believe, according to the working of His mighty power which He worked in Christ when He raised Him from the dead and seated Him at His right hand in the heavenly places, **far above all** principality and power and **might and dominion**, and every name that is named, not only in this age but also in that which is to come.
>
> And He put all things under His feet and gave Him to be head over all things to the church, which is His body, the fullness of Him who fills all in all" (Ephesians 1:17–23 emphasis added).

Now when you put together the information that is revealed in these few verses together with another discussion concerning what Scripture refers to as the first Adam and the second Adam, it becomes crystal clear who has dominion over God's creation today, and how that dominion is exercised. Listen carefully to the Apostle Paul as he says, "Nevertheless death reigned from Adam to Moses, even over those who had not sinned according to the likeness of the transgression of Adam, **who is a type of Him who was to come**" (Romans 5:14–15 Emphasis added). For this reason, Adam, the one who along with his wife Eve sinned against God and experienced spiritual death, is a picture of the One who would come and purchase back everything that they lost, including the spirit and dominion. The fullest explanation of this subject is found in chapter

---

[7] New International Version, 1978, 1999, International Bible Society.

fifteen of Paul's first letter to the Corinthian church where he makes a very detailed argument for life after physical death. Of course, we usually hear this chapter preached at a funeral to give family members of the deceased person hope. Nevertheless, it is also a clear explanation of who has dominion over God's creation today, and how the individual can avail themselves of it.

THE NATURE OF THE NEW SPIRIT

As I begin to draw this discussion of "beginnings" to a close, it becomes necessary to recognize another great truth that is the very foundation of the Gospel message. This great truth should make you shout "halleluiah" when you understand it with the help of the Holy Spirit. It is necessary to recognize that when God created Adam and Eve, He created a human spirit for them, which did connect them to God, but was not an eternal spirit and was subject to death. That is why God warned them that the spirit which He created for them was subject to death and would only remain with them until such time as they disobeyed God's clear command. This time, however, God did not give us a created Spirit, but he gave us an eternal Spirit. In fact, He gave us the very Holy Spirit, Who is the third member of the Godhead. Note this passage from Romans. "But if the Spirit of Him who raised Jesus from the dead dwells in you, He who raised Christ from the dead will also give life to your mortal bodies through His Spirit who dwells in you" (Romans 8:11). WOW! This must be central to our theological understanding of Scripture. God not only redeemed us by going to the cross for us and dying the death we earned for our sin, but as a gift for believing in Him and following Him in obedience, He then gives us of His very own eternal Spirit. Listen to Jesus as He describes the destiny of one who is born again of the Spirit of God: "Jesus said to her, "I am the resurrection and the life. He who believes in Me, though he may die, he shall live. And whoever lives and believes in Me shall never die. Do you believe this?" (John 11:25–26). And Jesus gets even clearer when He is answering a question about the resurrection when He said "nor can they die anymore, for they are equal to the angels and are sons of God, being sons of the resurrection (Luke 20:36).

I am painfully aware that this raises a very thorny question that has been a matter of controversy for many centuries on whether it is possible for one to lose their salvation once they are saved. I don't intend to answer that question here. I will say this, however, I do not intend on living my life in such a careless fashion as to find out if I can lose my salvation. The important truth that I want to leave with you as I close out chapter one is that the Spirit that we are born again with, when we choose to accept the sacrifice of Jesus Christ and believe in Him and confess Him as our Lord and Savior, is not some created spirit that is subject to death the moment we sin, but is the very Spirit of God, the very same Spirit that raised Jesus Christ from the dead (Romans 8:11). Praise God forevermore!

2

BAPTISM: WHAT IT IS
AND WHAT IT IS NOT

A DEFINITION OF THE WORD

Let me begin this important subject with an attempt to explain and define the word "baptism". It is a practice established in its present New Testament form by John the Baptist (Matthew 3:11; Luke 3:16; John 1:26-33). Although there is some evidence that the ritual was practiced long before him, he is the one who popularized the practice in Jesus's day. Although several forms of baptizing have been used by the church, it is generally understood to be the practice of applying water to the body of the person being baptized. John and Jesus along with His disciples practiced completely immersing the body of the person in water, symbolizing a person being buried and then raised to life again. Some Christians then began simply sprinkling water on the head of the individual. This practice began when it was thought that baptism was required for salvation and they began baptizing babies, which were too small to completely immerse, so they sprinkled water on them. Some Christians objected and most denominations today require adult baptism using the practice of complete immersion.

It is also noteworthy that the word is used to signify two, and one could rightly argue that a third is also mentioned in Scripture, completely different experiences and it is not always easy to determine which experience is being referred to when we see the word "baptize" used in Scripture. John, known as the Baptist, first introduced us to the second use of the word when he said

> There comes One after me who is mightier than I, whose sandal strap I am not worthy to stoop down and loose. I indeed baptized you with water, but He will baptize you with the Holy Spirit (Mark 1:7–8).

So now we need to recognize that there are two different baptisms that all serious Bible students need to grapple with; water baptism and spirit baptism. So, from this point on in Scripture we find several references to the term "baptize" and often it is evident which baptism is referred to but sometimes it is not so evident, and it seems to be up to the reader to discern which is referred to. Consequently, this confusion has caused much controversy and even division within the church over the centuries. In fact, there are whole denominations built around one understanding or the other. Now with these things clearly in mind, I want to tackle this subject and hopefully bring some reason to bear on the subject that has divided the church far too long, as well as discuss at some length the third baptism also mentioned.

THE TWO BAPTISMS REVEALED

Water Baptism

I want to discuss water baptism first because it in fact came first, although, I believe that one could rightly conclude that Spirit baptism was in the mind of God when he influenced people to be baptized in water. Water has always been a symbol of cleansing. For example, one of the pieces of furniture that Moses was commanded to build and place before the door of the tabernacle was the bronze laver (Exodus 30:18). This laver was filled with water and the priest had to wash himself with water each time he entered the Holy Place. Note at this point this was clearly a spiritual type[8] because God was intent on showing future generations an important truth. It is also important to understand these types when we tackle revelation in the New Testament. This becomes abundantly clear when we consider God's strict instruction to Moses as God showed him the pattern of things for the Tabernacle that were constructed in the wilderness after coming out of Egypt.

> And let them make Me a sanctuary, that I may dwell among them. 9 According to all that I show you, that is, the pattern of the tabernacle and the pattern of all its furnishings, just so you shall make it" (Exodus 25:8–9 and also note Exodus 25:40; Exodus 26:30; Acts 7:44).

This point is vital to not only baptism, but numerous other spiritual truths, even end-time events. It was absolutely essential that Moses construct the Tabernacle strictly according to the exact pattern shown to him on the mountain because God was revealing eternal truths that people would not begin to fully understand until the outpouring of the Holy Spirit at Pentecost, because, as Jesus taught in John 3, one cannot understand spiritual truth except with the Holy Spirit given at the new birth.

So, as noted above, the first piece of furniture that stood between the altar of sacrifice and the door of the Holy Place in the Tabernacle, was the bronze laver that was filled with water. This served a double purpose. Obviously, it was a rather messy situation to slaughter and sacrifice an animal and they would want to wash before proceeding with their obligations inside the tabernacle, but it also was a vital spiritual revelation of eternal significance. Notice carefully exactly what that water represented. Paul said this as he was explaining the marriage relationship which he concluded was really concerning Christ's relationship with His church. He said,

---

[8] A "type" in Scripture is a revelation of some truth that God is showing in some visible form (thing, person, or story) that is important for teaching deeper spiritual truth.

"that He might sanctify and cleanse her with the washing of water by the word, that He might present her to Himself a glorious church, not having spot or wrinkle or any such thing, but that she should be holy and without blemish" (Ephesians 5:26–27).

We must add one more piece to the puzzle to get the full picture of what water represents. Notice what Jesus's response to the Devil was when He was enduring 40 days of temptation in the wilderness. "But Jesus answered him, saying, "It is written, 'Man shall not live by bread alone, but by every word of God'" (Luke 4:4). Now one might object here because Jesus is clearly referring to food. But when one considers that drink is a substantial ingredient in food for the body, it is only reasonable to include water/the Word in this statement of Jesus. After all, most would understand without objection that food and drink go together because the human body cannot exist without both. So, we must rightly conclude that water represents the pure Word of God as revealed to us in Scripture.

Now to put that whole thought into plain words we must conclude that when anyone approaches a holy God, that one must be washed and purified by the Word of God. Not just in a ritual cleansing but remember that God commanded His people from the beginning to "… be holy; for I am holy…" (Leviticus 11:44). In other words, priests could not approach the Holy God until and unless they were washed pure in water (the Word of God). And before they even got to the laver and washed in water/the Word, they had to pass the brass altar on which had been sacrificed some animal to make atonement for their sins. It is imperative to understand that the attitude behind bringing this live animal, which had been inspected to ensure that it was without blemish, was repentance. In other words, they would recognize that they had sinned and repent for that sin in the form of bringing a substitute for themselves to have their sin forgiven. Now through repentance and a sacrifice for their sins, they were forgiven, they were washed in water/the Word of God, and now, and only now could they enter the presence of God.

We fast forward now to the New Testament and the ministry of John the Baptist. Notice what the ministry and message of John was. "John came baptizing in the wilderness and preaching a baptism of repentance for the remission of sins" (Mark 1:4). Ah, that sounds a lot like the ministry around the furniture at the tabernacle. The priest or person offering the sacrifice would stop first just inside the entrance of the courtyard to offer a sacrifice for their sins, and then wash at the bronze laver before entering the Tabernacle. Only now with John's ministry, it was becoming symbolic of something far greater to come. Remember, John the Baptist said as much when he explained the difference between the baptism of water and the baptism of the Spirit and the benefit each would offer when he said, "He must increase, but I must decrease" (John 3:30). In other words, the baptism that Jesus would offer would be much greater than the baptism that John offered. Nevertheless, they both involved repentance and the remission of sin. The former was a temporary remission until one sinned again and then they had to repeat the ritual and had to repent again and offer another sacrifice. But the latter was greater because it was a remission of all sins once and for all time. But the second baptism that John preached was far greater because it represented a once and for all time sacrifice that would never have to be repeated.

Of course, I assume that most readers at this point in the discussion would be asking the question; "So is water baptism still valid in the church today?" That is certainly a valid question and one which has caused a lot of controversy over the centuries of church history. I will answer that question later in this chapter, but first I want to discuss the second baptism that is mentioned in Scripture, Spirit baptism.

Spirit Baptism

In order to understand this discussion two things are absolutely essential. First, you will need to have read chapter one thoroughly and understood its content, and second, you will need to have been born-again of the Spirit. Let me begin this discussion by very briefly summarizing what we learned in chapter one. God created humankind in the beginning a three part being with a created spirit, a formed body, and the breath of life that was put into the body of the human form. Because this created being disobeyed God and sinned, as God had promised, their spirit died and left them only a two part being of the formed body and the breath of life. Because of this, they lost the dominion that God had given them and turned that dominion over to Lucifer or as he is better known today, Satan. However, even before creation, God had made plans to redeem these humans back to His intended place with dominion over His creation once again. Jesus revealed this plan by explaining that the details of this plan had been carefully kept secret since Eve and Adam sinned. Nevertheless, now that Jesus was here, He promised that when He went back to the Father that He would send the Holy Spirit who would reveal the secrets that had been kept secret since the beginning of time.

> But the Helper, the Holy Spirit, whom the Father will send in My name, He will teach you all things, and bring to your remembrance all things that I said to you (John 14:26).

And again, we need to be reminded of the conversation that Jesus had with Nicodemus recorded for us in John chapter 3. As you reread this conversation remember that John the Baptist had already said that he baptized in water, but that Jesus would baptize in or with the Holy Spirit (Mark 1:8). Consequently, there was no reason to not understand, except for the fact that, as Jesus tried to explain to him, it was impossible to understand this spiritual truth without this promised baptism in the Holy Spirit which Jesus referred to as a new birth experience. So, with these things clearly in mind let's read once again this whole conversation between Jesus and Nicodemus. (Because I have already printed out this entire Scripture elsewhere in the book, I will only reference it here – reread John 3:1–21.)

And it is vital as well to understand that the baptism in the Spirit involved even more according to Matthew's Gospel. Note that he said the same as Mark, Luke and John that Jesus would not baptize in water but would baptize in the Spirit, however, he added "fire" as part of the baptism that Jesus would offer.

> I indeed baptize you with water unto repentance, but He
> who is coming after me is mightier than I, whose sandals
> I am not worthy to carry. He will baptize you with the
> Holy Spirit and fire (Matthew 3:11).

That is significant, and we must understand what Jesus meant alongside our understanding of the baptism in the Holy Spirit. Without a clear understanding of this aspect of Spirit baptism, we will fall into error along with so many others who assume that the baptism in the Spirit is to enable them to speak in tongues, or the other equally false argument that baptism in the Spirit is really a meaningless thing for the church today.

Now the reason that this is so important to this conversation between Jesus and Nicodemus is because without a clear understanding, one will be led into gross error from the very beginning. As I pointed out in chapter one, there has been a lot of controversary, misunderstanding and gross error because people have not understood that the plan of salvation was kept a closely guarded secret in the Old Testament and in the attempt to build a doctrine based only on word studies in the Old Testament, many have come to wrong conclusions. One simply cannot build an accurate doctrine from unknown information. I am not trying to say that word studies in themselves are bad. If fact, the contrary is true. But my only point is that you cannot expect to find something that is hidden by God. Therefore, study words to discern important truth, along with New Testament revealed truth. The same principle applies here with the doctrine of the born-again experience and our discussion of the baptism in or with the Holy Spirit. Many people have read the account in Acts of the initial coming of the Holy Spirit and concluded that the purpose was so everyone could speak in tongues (Acts 2:1–4). In fact, whole denominations have been built around this experience. Some have even come to the erroneous conclusion that unless a person spoke in tongues upon receiving the Holy Spirit, they were not truly saved. And because this was such an obvious false doctrine, many who disagreed with that conclusion began to deny the experience altogether and build a case trying to prove that these gifts of the Spirit were only temporary gifts and are no longer valid for modern Christians.

I want to propose that both conclusions are wrong. When we read the whole conversation, we find that Jesus concludes the discussion with a clear explanation of why one must be born again and why God went to such lengths to bring it to pass. One of the most famous passages in Scripture is often memorized and quoted out of context. Remember that one of the foundational principles of Bible study is to always read and interpret Scripture in the context in which it is written. So, John 3:16 is not an isolated verse, but a clear explanation of just how important the born-again experience is. "For God so loved the world that He gave His only begotten Son, that whoever believes in Him should not perish but have everlasting life". Jesus said that it was so important to humankind to be born-again of the Spirit so they could understand the Scriptures and enter into God's kingdom, that in order to provide the way into this vital experience, God literally sacrificed His own Son and accepted that sacrifice as payment for Eve and Adam's sin. Notice the very next verse where Jesus explains the why behind God's choice to sacrifice His Only Son. "For God did not send His Son into the world to condemn the world, but that the world through Him might be saved" (John 3:17).

From this truth it should be abundantly clear that the purpose of the born-again experience is not only so that we can speak in tongues or exercise other gifts, but that we might have boldness to enter into God's presence (Acts 4:31), and as Jesus taught

> I still have many things to say to you, but you cannot bear them now. However, when He, the Spirit of truth, has come, He will guide you into all truth; for He will not speak on His own authority, but whatever He hears He will speak; and He will tell you things to come. He will glorify Me, for He will take of what is Mine and declare it to you. All things that the Father has are Mine. Therefore I said that He will take of Mine and declare it to you (John 16:12–15).

While we must realize that God gave the born-again church many and varied gifts – "When He ascended on high, He led captivity captive, And gave gifts to men....11 And He Himself gave some to be apostles, some prophets, some evangelists, and some pastors and teachers, (Ephesians 4:8, 11). And "There are diversities of gifts, but the same Spirit. 5 There are differences of ministries, but the same Lord. 6 And there are diversities of activities, but it is the same God who works all in all" (1 Corinthians 12:4–6). While the gifts are vital for God's people to have and use, we must conclude however, that the sole purpose of giving the Holy Spirit to a believer when they come humbly and with repentance to the Father, was so that that "whoever believes in Him should not perish but have eternal life" (John 3:15). Nevertheless, it is also vital to understand that "For the gifts and the calling of God are irrevocable" (Romans 11:29). In other words, we cannot randomly claim that the gifts of the Spirit are not valid today, but rather understand that the gifts are a bonus that comes with the baptism in the Holy Spirit, not the sole purpose of the experience. Consequently, it is the duty of God's people to understand that God did not change His mind and take the gifts that He gave away from the church, but rather learn what the gifts are for and use them properly. Just because many people misuse, and in some cases, abuse the gifts, does not make them invalid. Many people misuse and even abuse a physical gift that they may have received, but it is still their gift. For example, if someone gave you a brand-new car, you have the right to do with that car anything you choose. You can even take it out and race it and wreck it the first day you have it if you are foolish enough to do such a thing. Now, the one who gave it to you might be upset with you and not give you anymore gifts, but it was yours to do with as you pleased. Once God gives you a gift, it is yours to do with what you want. Now, we must acknowledge another equally valid truth, and that is that we are responsible for the gifts God gives to us. Yes, it is ours and we are free to use it, or put it on the shelf and ignore it, or even to abuse the gift and use it in an inappropriate way, but God does not remove it from us for this conduct. There are consequences for misusing God's gifts, but He does not take them away from us just because we misuse them. This should motivate us to find out how God intends for His gifts to be used and use them properly, because there are rewards for the proper use and consequences for the misuse of them. But to deny them is not the answer.

BAPTISM IN FIRE

I feel compelled to discuss this topic separate from Spirit baptism because it is only mentioned this once and is often neglected in the debate about baptism in general. Consequently, I believe it is vital for a Christian to understand what Matthew was speaking about. I believe that one of the reasons it has been so neglected in theological discussions is because it flies in the face of most modern 21st century doctrines. While modern people usually think of hell when one mentions fire in a spiritual context, it becomes obvious when one "rightly divides" (2 Timothy 2:15) the relevant scriptural references, that it has a much broader meaning.

Consider, for example this use of the term: "The words of the Lord are pure words, Like silver tried in a furnace of earth, Purified seven times" (Psalm 12:6). And further, consider this familiar verse from the book of Revelation: "I counsel you to buy from Me gold refined in the fire …" (3:18). So now it begins to become obvious that the use of the term "fire" has a much deeper and more spiritual meaning. I propose that this is the use of the word when Matthew said that Jesus's baptism in the Holy Spirit would include fire. When we read the context of the verse in Revelation that I just quoted, you will discover that this principle becomes clear.

> I counsel you to buy from Me gold refined in the fire, that you may be rich; and white garments, that you may be clothed, that the shame of your nakedness may not be revealed; and anoint your eyes with eye salve, that you may see. As many as I love, I rebuke and chasten. Therefore be zealous and repent. Behold, I stand at the door and knock. If anyone hears My voice and opens the door, I will come in to him and dine with him, and he with Me. To him who overcomes I will grant to sit with Me on My throne, as I also overcame and sat down with My Father on His throne.
>
> "He who has an ear, let him hear what the Spirit says to the churches""
> (Revelation 3:18–22).

Of course, gold (that is only made pure by fire) refers to the purity and costliness of God's nature and since we are commanded in Leviticus 19:1–2 "And the Lord spoke to Moses, saying, 2 "Speak to all the congregation of the children of Israel, and say to them: 'You shall be holy, for I the Lord your God am holy". And because no one is holy, nor can be in their own effort, God must work righteousness into us by His Holy Spirit. Notice that John said in this verse, "as many as I love, I rebuke and chasten." This concept is repeated throughout the Scriptures in both the Old Testament as well as the New Testament. Consider these two verses:

> You should know in your heart that as a man chastens his son, so the Lord your God chastens you" (Deuteronomy 8:5).

> For whom the Lord loves He chastens, And scourges every son whom He receives." If you endure chastening, God deals with you as with sons; for what son is there whom a father does not chasten? But if you are without chastening, of which all have become partakers, then you are illegitimate and not sons. Furthermore, we have had human fathers who corrected us, and we paid them respect. Shall we not much more readily be in subjection to the Father of spirits and live? For they indeed for a few days chastened us as seemed best to them, but He for our profit, that we may be partakers of His holiness. Now no chastening seems to be joyful for the present, but painful; nevertheless, afterward it yields the peaceable fruit of righteousness to those who have been trained by it" (Hebrews 12:6–11).

The conclusion of the matter then is twofold; 1) God gives us as a free gift, the very righteousness of Jesus Christ so we can today, even in our sinful condition, come boldly before the throne of grace as completely righteous in God's sight, and 2) at the same time, He is committed to working righteousness into our lives and he does that through the furnace of affliction. Notice the teaching in these verses;

> "Behold, I have refined you, but not as silver; I have tested you in the furnace of affliction" (Isaiah 48:10).

And,

> "I will bring the one-third through the fire, Will refine them as silver is refined, And test them as gold is tested. They will call on My name, And I will answer them. I will say, 'This is My people'; And each one will say, 'The Lord is my God'" (Zechariah 13:9I).

And of course, we must include the words of Job who experienced the refining process of the Lord. "But He knows the way that I take; When He has tested me, I shall come forth as gold", which, of course, is accomplished through fire (Job 23:10).

Let me summarize then what we have learned so far concerning the baptism of fire. All of the verses that I have quoted need to be tied together so we can have a full picture of what God is wanting to teach us. God has always been intent on having a holy people in every way and in every area of life. He began with Adam and Eve and when they sinned, He chose a people through Abraham to deal with in a special way to bring them to holiness. His intention was that they "shall be to Me a kingdom of priests and a holy nation" (Exodus 19:6). God's method of dealing with this special chosen people was through blessings for obedience and hardships or sufferings for disobedience (see Deuteronomy 28 and Joshua 23:15). When God's chosen people, Israel, failed miserably at God's command to be holy and a priesthood to the nations by becoming more wicked than the pagan world around them, He brought forth His Son, Jesus, who was actually promised in the very beginning to Abraham (Galatians 3:16). In fact, when we put it all together we find that God's goal for His people has not changed one bit. Because we find Peter repeating God's heart to make His chosen people a kingdom of priests. "(Y)ou also, as living stones, are being built up a spiritual house, a holy priesthood, to offer up spiritual sacrifices acceptable to God through Jesus Christ.... But you are a chosen generation, a royal priesthood, a holy nation, His own special people, that you may proclaim the praises of Him who called you out of darkness into His marvelous light" (1 Peter 2:5 & 9).

And further, God has not changed His method of dealing with His people either. This is where the baptism in fire appears. Notice the very clear teaching of both Jesus and the apostles in the New Testament. First the words of the writer of the book of Hebrews.

> If you endure chastening, God deals with you as with sons; for what son is there whom a father does not chasten? But if you are without chastening, of which all have become partakers, then you are illegitimate and not sons. Furthermore, we have had human fathers who corrected us, and we paid them respect. Shall we not much more readily be in subjection to the Father of spirits and live? For they indeed for a few days chastened us as seemed best to them, but He for our profit, that we may be partakers of His holiness. Now no chastening seems to be joyful for the present, but painful; nevertheless, afterward it yields the peaceable fruit of righteousness to those who have been trained by it (Hebrews 12:7–11).

And of course, we find Jesus Himself speaking to the church at Laodicea as recorded by the beloved apostle John. I will use the whole letter to the Laodicean church so we are sure to understand the context of what Jesus is saying.

> 'These things says the Amen, the Faithful and True Witness, the Beginning of the creation of God: "I know your works, that you are neither cold nor hot. I could wish you were cold or hot. So then, because you are lukewarm, and neither cold nor hot, I will vomit you out of My mouth. Because you say, 'I am rich, have become

wealthy, and have need of nothing' — and do not know that you are wretched, miserable, poor, blind, and naked — I counsel you to buy from Me gold refined in the fire, that you may be rich; and white garments, that you may be clothed, that the shame of your nakedness may not be revealed; and anoint your eyes with eye salve, that you may see. As many as I love, I rebuke and chasten. Therefore be zealous and repent. Behold, I stand at the door and knock. If anyone hears My voice and opens the door, I will come in to him and dine with him, and he with Me. To him who overcomes I will grant to sit with Me on My throne, as I also overcame and sat down with My Father on His throne.

"He who has an ear, let him hear what the Spirit says to the churches"""
(Revelation 3:14–22).

Notice that in both of these passages the sufferings of chastening are for a very specific purpose – to bring about change. Isaiah the prophet agrees: "Behold, I have refined you, but not as silver; I have tested you in the furnace of affliction" (48:10).

Now I could quote many other verses to make this very important point, but please understand that, yes, we are saved by faith, and then we are given the gift of righteousness so that we can "... come boldly to the throne of grace..." (Hebrews 4:16). Nevertheless, God is still determined to work righteousness into us, that is, into our daily conduct and behavior, and His method of doing that is through chastening, sufferings, the furnace of afflictions, and any other means that He deems necessary to mature us in His Spirit. You see, God has not changed His mind. This is the fallacy that makes up so many false doctrines. Why? Because "... the gifts and the calling of God are irrevocable" (Romans 11:29). God simply does not change His mind. His purposes and plans are always the same. The only thing that has changed from the Old Testament days of living under the Law of Moses is His approach. He used to work from the outside in, that is the people had to live by the Law, but now, He is working from the inside out, that is through the Holy Spirit which He gives to those who come to Him humbly and with repentance. When one rightly understands all of Scripture, however, you will quickly discover that God did not, in fact, change His mind at all, He simply put His people under a "tutor" for a period of time and then in Christ Jesus, He returned to His original plan of working through the Spirit, that is that part of the human being that died because of the sin of Eve and Adam. Listen to Paul explain this truth for us; "Therefore the law was our tutor to bring us to Christ, that we might be justified by faith. But after faith has come, we are no longer under a tutor" (Galatians 3:24–25).

NEW TESTAMENT BAPTISM

This now brings us to the all-important question, "So what is the baptism that is valid for today's church members?" There has been an enormous amount of diversity on how people have answered that question over the centuries of church history. Some, believing that water baptism is the element that saves a person, will therefore insist on baptizing people with water at birth or very early in life, called by most "infant baptism". Of course, the idea is that if water baptism is necessary for salvation, then one must be baptized in water very young so in the event that thy die young, they can still go to heaven. Others insist that water baptism is valid only when one reaches the age of "consent" which in itself causes controversy because then you have to decide the age of consent or accountability. This is called by most "adult" baptism. The idea here, of course, is that yes, baptism is necessary for salvation but because one must personally choose Jesus as his or her Savior, they cannot have a valid baptism until they reach the age where they can make an informed choice for themselves. Then, there are even some who deny that water baptism is even valid in the New Testament era because the only baptism valid in New Testament time is Spirit baptism. Therefore, we must again, rightly divide the Scripture to see what the truth of the matter is.

I want to begin this part of the discussion with a very curious event in the Book of Acts. It involves Peter's experience with his first Gentile converts. Understand that this event took place several years into the life of the New Testament Church. Peter had been evangelizing only Jews and not certain yet that God was even interested in the Gentiles. Consequently, God gave him a very clear vision to open up his understanding to Old Testament prophesy concerning God's heart for the Gentiles. Now Peter was faithful to go but was very uncertain about what would happen once he got there. Listen to the account;

> While Peter was still speaking these words, the Holy Spirit fell upon all those who heard the word. And those of the circumcision who believed were astonished, as many as came with Peter, because the gift of the Holy Spirit had been poured out on the Gentiles also (Acts 10:44–45).

Now that is fairly clear to us today, but it was world changing event for Peter and the Jewish converts, because this was the first time people who were not Jews were offered the gospel message of salvation and everyone involved was "astonished" because they did not know that a non-Jew could be saved. As we read further of the account, we find that immediately upon receiving the promised baptism in or the filling of the Spirit, Peter then had them all baptized in water. This is significant for two reasons. First, it gives us the proper order of baptism, that is Spirit baptism first and water baptism following, and second it answers the important question of which baptism is necessary for salvation. I believe it is also significant that when Peter, a few days later had to answer for this event before a council of Jewish leaders, he only mentions the baptism in the Spirit and never mentioned the second baptism in water. Notice what Peter recounts to this Jewish council in Acts chapter 11, only a few days after the experience with these Gentile converts. After explaining in some detail why he went to them in the first place and what took place once he arrived, he has this to say:

And as I begin to speak, the Holy Spirit fell upon them, as upon us at the beginning. Then I remembered the word of the Lord, how He said, 'John indeed baptized with water, but you shall be baptized with the Holy Spirit.' If therefore God gave them the same gift as He gave us when we believed on the Lord Jesus Christ, who was I that I could withstand God? (Acts 11:15–17).

Notice that he does not even mention the fact that he baptized them in water after they had received the baptism in the Holy Spirit. It is evident that Peter thought that the filling (baptism) in the Spirit was the important event that took place. In other words, Peter, after several years of not fully comprehending, finally understood Jesus's words when he uttered the words "then I remembered the word of the Lord, how He said, 'John indeed baptized with water, but you shall be baptized with the Holy Spirit.'" Remember that this is the baptism or new birth that Jesus told Nicodemus about, and it was this experience that was necessary in order to understand the Kingdom, then, and only then would it be appropriate to engage in the second baptism, a baptism in water. I think that it is also significant that after Peter uttered this account in Acts 11, we do not see water baptism referred to again. Now we do know from church history that the church continued baptizing people in water throughout church history even up to the current day. However, we do not hear of it again in the New Testament. It is also very interesting to note that while water baptism has remained central to the Christian movement throughout history, it is Spirit baptism that has generated the most controversy and has even disappeared from church experience for long periods of time. And, of course, that would make sense, since the church has a sworn enemy who desires to destroy or pervert anything and everything that is genuine concerning the gospel, salvation and truth.

So now let me summarize what we have learned and suggest a theology of baptism that is both biblically and historically correct. There are hints of water baptism as old as the law of Moses. Remember our discussion concerning the brass laver that contained a supply of water at the door of the tabernacle that the priest had to wash himself at before entering the tabernacle? That was a very vivid picture of the necessity of approaching God only after repentance and a complete cleansing. God wanted the priest (us) to know that after the sacrifice that had been made on the bronze altar (for us at the ascension of Jesus and the outpouring of the Holy Spirit), that they were washed clean from all their sin and could then approach their Holy God with confidence. John the Baptist also preached a baptism of repentance. Remember his words, "I indeed baptize you with water unto repentance, but He who is coming after me is mightier than I, whose sandals I am not worthy to carry. He will baptize you with the Holy Spirit and fire" (Matthew 3:11). So, it is very clear that the baptism in water was for repentance. In other words, once they repented of their sins, then they were eligible to come and be baptized in water. Thus, showing the transition from animal sacrifice for remission of their sin to the real sacrifice for sin that was then walking among them and would soon die for the sins of the world, paving the way for the real baptism, the baptism necessary for salvation, emersion in the Holy Spirit. But water baptism remains as a very important event in the life of a saved Christian to demonstrate in a very real and visible way what happened spiritually at the new birth.

"Therefore we were buried with Him through baptism into death, that just as Christ was raised from the dead by the glory of the Father, even so we also should walk in newness of life" (Romans 6:4). And a similar description in Colossians 2:12–13; "buried with Him in baptism, in which you also were raised with Him through faith in the working of God, who raised Him from the dead." So water baptism is a clear picture of what happens at the moment of salvation. We die to our old self and of course once dead, you are buried as you go under the water, and once dead we are raised with Jesus, brought up out of the water, and on our way to a new life with Christ in His kingdom.

THE CONCLUSION OF THE WHOLE MATTER

The Scripture makes it clear what the two baptisms are all about and what the correct understanding of them should be. First, of course, is repentance, that is a complete turning one's life over to Christ, our Passover lamb, and allowing Him to fill you with His very own Spirit and thus, bring you forever into His eternal family, which, of course, we in Christian jargon call salvation. So now that the person is completely saved and forgiven of his/her sins, there is a need for some action on the part of the new believer to show and to personally understand what happened to him/her at that filling (baptism) in the Holy Spirit. And it seems very logical and very clear that that action on the part of the new believer would be water baptism. Water baptism, while it is not necessary for salvation (one is filled with the Spirit at salvation), it will be desired to declare publicly what happened when filled with the Spirit. In other words, at salvation and the filling with the Holy Spirit they were completely washed clean, given the gift of righteousness purchased for them by Christ's sacrifice, and are now eligible to ". . . come boldly to the throne of grace, that we may obtain mercy and find grace to help in time of need" (Hebrews 4:16). And not only that, it is also a very visible picture of a vital spiritual truth. "Therefore we were buried with Him through baptism into death, that just as Christ was raised from the dead by the glory of the Father, even so we also should walk in newness of life" (Romans 6:4). Paul insists that water baptism is a wonderful picture of what happens when we are saved and born-again by being filled with the Spirit. We literally enter into the death of Christ and therefore the penalty of our sin, death, was paid and now we are free from the law that demanded the penalty of death for our sin, and free to live by the righteousness of faith. Listen as Paul teaches about this truth; "For Moses writes about the righteousness which is of the law, "The man who does those things shall live by them." (Romans 10:5). But the born-again Christian, has a new way to live;

> I have been crucified with Christ; it is no longer I who
> live, but Christ lives in me; and the life which I now live
> in the flesh I live by faith in the Son of God, who loved
> me and gave Himself for me" (Galatians 2:20).

In other words, I am saved by repentance toward God and He then fills me with His very own Spirit, called the rebirth experience, or as many refer to it, being born-again. That experience attaches us eternally to Christ, whose righteousness we are given as a gift, thereby fully paying the price for our sin. We are literally buried with Christ at our water baptism, and immediately identify with the work He has accomplished for us by raising us up from burial to a new life in Christ. What a wonderful, vital, necessary picture we get when we submit to water baptism. We must understand as Christians, first comes repentance immediately followed by Spirit baptism, then comes water baptism which is a clear declaration of our repentance and association with or in Christ's death and resurrection where we are raised never to die again. Spirit baptism is absolutely necessary for salvation (John 3), but water baptism, while not necessary for salvation, is a vital experience that shows us very graphically what Christ accomplished for us and what truly happened at Spirit baptism. Some people because of this truth, have denied the necessity of water baptism, however I suggest that it, too, is a vital experience that every born-again believer should have. Not because it saves you, because if you have been born-again of the Spirit, you are already saved, but because as humans we need the picture of the reality of what happened at Spirit baptism. It is similar to the Communion that most Christian churches celebrate often. Taking Communion does not save us but helps us remember what Christ has accomplished for us. "And He took bread, gave thanks and broke it, and gave it to them, saying, "This is My body which is given for you; do this in remembrance of Me" (Luke 22:19). In like manner, water baptism, while it does not save you, is a vital visual reminder of exactly what Christ has accomplished for you and that "I have been crucified with Christ; it is no longer I who live, but Christ lives in me; and the life which I now live in the flesh I live by faith in the Son of God, who loved me and gave Himself for me" (Galatians 2:20).

3

MARRIAGE, HUMAN RELATIONSHIPS, AND HUMAN SEXUALITY

Marriage is without a doubt the most important human relationship that the Bible speaks about. After all, it is the relationship that God describes as His desired relationship with His redeemed people. Therefore, I want to study this subject in some detail. And since we have a command that runs throughout the whole of Scripture to "love your neighbor as yourself", we also need to consider all human relationships outside the marriage bond. And, of course, in all three of these categories of relationships, there is the subject of human sexuality, that needs looked at in some detail as well. This discussion becomes all the more relevant when one considers the 21st century debate about gender, gender roles, and the homosexual lifestyle that permeates societies around the world including the church. So, while it is with some fear and trepidation that I approach this subject, knowing as well, that no matter what conclusions I might come to, there will be those who disagree. Nevertheless, I feel compelled to add my understanding to the subject.

GOD'S PLAN FOR MARRIAGE

Of course, the classic New Testament understanding of marriage is given to us by the anonymous writer of Hebrews: "Marriage is honorable among all, and the bed undefiled; but fornicators and adulterers God will judge" (Hebrews 13:4). This seems clear enough, nevertheless, many still misunderstand God's intent with the relationship of marriage. For example, the breakup of this most basic relationship runs rampant throughout the world, including the church. Moses had to face this issue with Israel and even included guidelines in the Law concerning how the marriage relationship should be viewed. Divorce has always been an issue in any society and the church has weighed in on the debate in various ways throughout history.

It would seem that one should begin this discussion with the question, "Is it all right for a man to have more than one wife?" Now this might not seem like a relevant question in the 21st century, however, it has been a question asked periodically throughout history. When one gives serious consideration to the Scriptures, it becomes obvious that God intended marriage to be strictly and only between one man and one woman as a lifetime relationship, as long as they both shall live. The classic Scripture that shows God's purpose for the marriage relationship is found at their creation. "Therefore a man (singular) shall leave his father and mother and be joined to his wife (singular), and they shall become one flesh" (Genesis 2:23), the words "singular" my explanation. And then just a few years later we see the son of Cain taking two wives, although God doesn't take kindly to it.

> Then Lamech took for himself two wives: the name of one was Adah, and the name of the second was Zillah. And Adah bore Jabal. He was the father of those who dwell in tents and have livestock. His brother's name was Jubal. He was the father of all those who play the harp and flute. And as for Zillah, she also bore Tubal-Cain, an instructor of every craftsman in bronze and iron. And the sister of Tubal-Cain was Naamah.

Then Lamech said to his wives:

"Adah and Zillah, hear my voice;
Wives of Lamech, listen to my speech!
For I have killed a man for wounding me,
Even a young man for hurting me.
If Cain shall be avenged sevenfold,
Then Lamech seventy-sevenfold" (Genesis 4:19–24).

Scripture moves on to the history of Adam and Eve's third son, Seth and continues quickly to the story of Noah. People began to multiply greatly on the Earth and wickedness also greatly increased, including people not honoring the marriage relationship and taking multiple wives; sexual perversion quickly becomes the norm. However, there was one person who found favor in God's eyes: "Noah was a just man, perfect in his generations. Noah walked with God" (Genesis 6:9b). It is important to notice that among other things that caused God to testify that Noah was a just man was the fact that, he as well as his three sons, all had only one wife and all indications were that they were faithful to their wives for their lifetime. Of course, we do see one flaw in his son Ham, but it doesn't seem to be about another woman, but something concerning his father.

After the flood people began to multiply again on the face of the earth. They once again began getting more and more corrupt and sin once again reigned on the earth. We find this documented both in the Old Testament as well as the New Testament where we see the Apostle Paul quote parts of Psalm 14 and Psalm 53 in his letter to the Romans chapter 3.

The fool has said in his heart,
"There is no God."
They are corrupt, and have done abominable iniquity;
There is none who does good.
2 God looks down from heaven upon the children of men,
To see if there are any who understand, who seek God.
3 Every one of them has turned aside;

> They have together become corrupt;
> There is none who does good,
> No, not one (Psalm 53:1–3).

It was this condition that caused people to become corrupt in every area of life. Consequently, a lot of people began taking multiple wives and sexual corruption of all kinds began to show up in culture. Most of God's people were caught up in this corruption but because of God's grace and longsuffering, He put up with it. Many times throughout history, some people have argued that having multiple wives was the "norm". And in some ways they were right, but just because it was normal in culture, it does not equate to being right in God's eyes. A careful reading of the Old Testament reveals that idol worship was normal behavior for both Israel and the Gentiles, but nobody argues that it was acceptable to God.

GOD'S VIEW OF THOSE WHO DO NOT FIT THE "NORM"

Now we must move on to a subject that is difficult at best to address because there is so much controversary and it seems like no one is neutral on the subject. One could probably assume correctly that everyone has someone in their family or close circle of friends who does not fit the "norm" when it comes to personality and lifestyle. Sexual deviation from the "norm" is a large part of human nature and has been since the "fall" of Adam and Eve in the Garden. It is evident from a cursory reading of the Bible that in the beginning God created His human creation as a male and a female with nothing in-between.

> Then God said, "Let Us make man in Our image, according to Our likeness; let them have dominion over the fish of the sea, over the birds of the air, and over the cattle, over all the earth and over every creeping thing that creeps on the earth." So God created man in His

own image; in the image of God He created him; male
and female He created them. (Genesis 1:26–27)

It was not long however, that humankind began to deviate from this "norm" and began to have multiple wives and to have sexual relations outside God's command to cling to his wife. People eventually began religious activity centered around the sexual act and it was not unknown for some people to even engage in sexual activity with animals. It must be noted nevertheless that God strictly condemned such abnormal sexual activity outside of marriage. It seems like He did tolerate men having more than one wife, but sexual activity outside of the marriage bond was always condemned by God. God was very clear as well that sexual activity between men or with any animal was strictly forbidden, and in the Law, brought the death penalty. Notice what the Law said:

You shall not lie with a male as with a woman. It is an abomination. Nor shall you mate with any animal, to defile yourself with it. Nor shall any woman stand before an animal to mate with it. It is perversion.

'Do not defile yourselves with any of these things; for by all these the nations are defiled, which I am casting out before you. (Leviticus 18:22–25).

In the New Testament most Christians will turn to Paul's discussion in Romans chapter one to defend their position against certain kinds of sexual perversion especially homosexual activity. And, if one is to be honest with Scripture, will have to agree that sexual activity outside the marriage union is considered rebellion in God's eyes in the New Testament as well as the Old Testament.

Upon close examination of Scripture, it would seem that it is the sexual behavior that God is concerned about rather than the "orientation", that is the attraction to a certain sex, or the personal characteristics of a person's personality, such as "feminine" or "masculine" behavior as described by cultural "norms. In other words, a man who seems to display feminine characteristics as understood by the dominate culture or a woman who displays masculine characteristics, as understood by the dominate culture in his or her personal life and behavior. Scripture is very clear on the subject, but because of so many centuries of bias and wrong teaching, one will have to follow the following argument very closely to understand God's heart. I believe that for far too long the church has shunned those who are "different" and I urge the reader to read the whole argument before shutting off your mind to what the Bible says. Engage your mind but most of all your reason to see what God's heart is toward those among us who are "different" and don't display the characteristics that we recognize as clearly male or female.

I want to begin by sharing a familiar story from the Book of Acts.

> Now an angel of the Lord spoke to Philip, saying, "Arise and go toward the south along the road which goes down from Jerusalem to Gaza." This is desert. So he arose and went. And behold, a man of Ethiopia, a eunuch of great authority under Candace the queen of the Ethiopians, who had charge of all her treasury, and had come to Jerusalem to worship, was returning. And sitting in his chariot, he was reading Isaiah the prophet. Then the Spirit said to Philip, "Go near and overtake this chariot."

> So Philip ran to him, and heard him reading the prophet Isaiah, and said, "Do you understand what you are reading?"

> And he said, "How can I, unless someone guides me?" And he asked Philip to come up and sit with him. The place in the Scripture which he read was this:

> "He was led as a sheep to the slaughter;

> And as a lamb before its shearer is silent,

So He opened not His mouth.

In His humiliation His justice was taken away,

And who will declare His generation?

For His life is taken from the earth."

So the eunuch answered Philip and said, "I ask you, of whom does the prophet say this, of himself or of some other man?" Then Philip opened his mouth, and beginning at this Scripture, preached Jesus to him. 36 Now as they went down the road, they came to some water. And the eunuch said, "See, here is water. What hinders me from being baptized?"

Then Philip said, "If you believe with all your heart, you may."

And he answered and said, "I believe that Jesus Christ is the Son of God."

So he commanded the chariot to stand still. And both Philip and the eunuch went down into the water, and he baptized him. Now when they came up out of the water, the Spirit of the Lord caught Philip away, so that the eunuch saw him no more; and he went on his way rejoicing. But Philip was found at Azotus. And passing through, he preached in all the cities till he came to Caesarea. (Acts 8:26–40).

Why begin with this story? Well, for two very good reasons. Number one, is that it is an exciting story of God's providence in reaching out to an unreached people, and number two, it records God's use of a person who did not meet the "normal" cultural standards for being a man. In fact, a man in his condition was forbidden from any kind of service in the Law of Moses.

> And the Lord spoke to Moses, saying, "Speak to Aaron, saying: 'No man of your descendants in succeeding generations, who has any defect, may approach to offer the bread of his God. For any man who has a defect shall not approach: a man blind or lame, who has a marred face or any limb too long, a man who has a broken foot or broken hand, or is a hunchback or a dwarf, or a man who has a defect in his eye, or eczema or scab, **or is a eunuch** (Leviticus 21:16–21 emphasis added).

And it is clear that many Ethiopians claim that the Treasurer eunuch probably introduced the Christian faith when he returned to Ethiopia from his pilgrimage to Jerusalem well before the fourth century, but Christianity did not become the officially recognized religion until the reign of King Ezana in 341 AD.

So, the question becomes, "Can God use a "eunuch" in His service today?" I believe that most of us can understand that the sexual revolution of the past 20 years has clouded the real issue for the Church. The world has been sold the idea that if you are a man and you are not attracted to women, then you must be attracted to men, therefore you should have the right to have sex with a man instead of a woman. And whether we agree with it or not, we all know that the Bible strictly forbids such behavior, however, I don't believe that that is the issue at all. America as well as a number of other countries have legalized sex between people of the same sex, in fact in America the current debate is about having sex with animals. In some Arab countries this is already legal. The Bible is very clear that such behavior is strictly forbidden. Any kind of sexual perversion is forbidden by Scripture. So, let's look at Scripture and see what we learn.

We begin this discussion by looking at what at first glance seems like another subject altogether – marriage and divorce. Consider this conversation between Jesus and His disciples:

The Pharisees also came to Him, testing Him, and saying to Him, "Is it lawful for a man to divorce his wife for just any reason?"

And He answered and said to them, "Have you not read that He who made them at the beginning 'made them male and female,' and said, 'For this reason a man shall leave his father and mother and be joined to his wife, and the two shall become one flesh'? So then, they are no longer two but one flesh. Therefore what God has joined together, let not man separate."

They said to Him, "Why then did Moses command to give a certificate of divorce, and to put her away?"

He said to them, "Moses, because of the hardness of your hearts, permitted you to divorce your wives, but from the beginning it was not so. And I say to you, whoever divorces his wife, except for sexual immorality, and marries another, commits adultery; and whoever marries her who is divorced commits adultery."

His disciples said to Him, "If such is the case of the man with his wife, it is better not to marry." (Matthew 19:3–10).

Notice first of all that the question was not even a sincere question, but the religious leaders were simply "testing Him" trying to set a trap to criticize Him. However, Jesus recognized their hypocrisy and answered them in a way they did not expect, and I suspect in a way most Christians today wouldn't expect either. Notice as well that Jesus was very specific in His answer concerning the marriage arrangement. He said that "the two" involved in the marriage "shall become one flesh". Two, not many, not several, only two, the one man and his one wife. Second, they are not to separate or divorce. God did allow it because of "the hardness of your hearts", but that was not God's design or plan for marriage. It was to be a lifelong relationship between one man and one woman.

Now, one other important truth we need to consider. Remember that the most important principle of Bible study is to understand every Scripture properly, one must read it in context. And so far we have not quoted this conversation in its whole context. If we were to stop reading at verse ten, we could settle on the above conclusions. However, Jesus did not stop his explanation at verse ten, but He continued responding to the question posed to Him by the Pharisees. And this is very important information for us to consider when we are judging people who are "different" from us. Listen carefully as Jesus now talks about those who don't fit nicely into our Christian worldview as men who are only attracted to women and women who are not attracted to men. The disciples came to the conclusion that if what Jesus said about marriage was true, then "it is better not to marry." Notice that Jesus begins His response to His disciple's response with the word "but".

> But He said to them, "All cannot accept this saying, but only those to whom it has been given: For there are eunuchs who were born thus from their mother's womb, and there are eunuchs who were made eunuchs by men, and there are eunuchs who have made themselves eunuchs for the kingdom of heaven's sake. He who is able to accept it, let him accept it." (Matthew 19:11–12).

Pay special attention to Jesus's final words on this subject. "There are eunuchs who have made themselves eunuchs for the sake of the kingdom of heaven. Let the one who is able to receive this receive it" (v. 12). Remember what Paul taught about the various categories of people as he grappled with biases in his day.

> There is neither Jew nor Greek, there is neither slave nor free, there is neither male nor female; for you are all one in Christ Jesus. And if you are Christ's, then you

are Abraham's seed, and heirs according to the promise.
(Galatians 3:28–29)

Christ's appeal to creation and His restrictions on the lawful grounds for divorce (Matthew 19:3–9) rebuke any desire to find loopholes in the marriage laws in order to escape unions that sinners find unfulfilling. Marriage is to be cherished wholeheartedly, not to be dispensed with as we in vain attempt to find "happiness" outside of God's gracious law. Husbands and wives are called to obey the Lord together and work tirelessly to become one flesh physically, emotionally, and spiritually by guarding and renewing their relationship (Genesis 2:24–25).

And we need to understand clearly that God holds us all, male, female, eunuch, all to the same moral standard. In other words, any sexual activity outside of the marriage union is strictly forbidden by God.

But most of us will still ask the question; "Why does God make eunuchs?" Well, I don't know if God purposely made people like that or if it is a result of the fall of creation spoken about by Paul in his letter to the Romans "For the creation was subjected to futility, not willingly, but because of Him who subjected it in hope; because the creation itself also will be delivered from the bondage of corruption into the glorious liberty of the children of God" (Romans 8:20–22). Whatever the reason or the source we as Christians need to deal with it in a godly and biblical manner.

As anyone who listens to or reads the news lately, the hot topic is concerning the many and varied gender related controversies. This news causes a mixture of reactions inside of me. I am tempted to simply dismiss and criticize the hype it all has created. Nevertheless, at the same time, I've met people who were clearly anatomically female and hormonally male and vice-versa. I've seen boys who acted completely like girls at too young an age for it to be a product of socialization. Many social conservatives assume transgender identity was invented in the sexual revolution. But what if it's always been around among people who have lived in the shadows? What if God has created some people not male or female, but male-and-female? Jesus says that He can.[9]

In Matthew 19, Jesus is responding to a question about divorce. In verses 4–6, he lays out the traditional understanding of gender presented by the Torah. God created people male and female. Men are commanded to leave their fathers and mothers in order to become one flesh with a woman, the implication being that their genders perfectly complement one another in a way that they can be united. Many preachers have used Matthew 19 as a text to preach in defense of traditional marriage, which works as long as you stop before verse 10, because that's where Jesus' disciples say, "If this is the situation between a husband and wife, it is better not to marry." Then Jesus says that his disciples should emulate eunuchs, whom he categorizes into three types: "There are eunuchs who **_were born that way_**, and there are eunuchs who **_have been made eunuchs by others_**—and there are those **_who choose to live like eunuchs_** for the sake of the kingdom of heaven" (Matthew 9:12 emphasis added).

Eunuchs in the ancient world were men who were castrated so that they could guard the king's wives and concubines without being tempted to have sex with them. They were thus men who lacked the one definitive aspect of manhood. A eunuch who is "born that way" is definitively neither male nor female, whether it is a question of their physical makeup or if it is simply their emotional/mental state. In other words, some men simple do not have the physical capability to perform the traditional role of a man with a woman, while others simply do not have any "inclination" or "desire" for a relationship with a person of the opposite sex. The use of the term eunuch signifies simply one who is incapable of impregnating a woman. Although I believe that one could rightly argue that He is referring to males and females both who might not fit the "normal". Why would God create someone like that if His entire purpose in creating men and women is to marry them off and make babies with them? The problem is that Jesus's words don't always fit very neatly into the agenda

---

[9] Much of the material for this discussion on eunuchs is from a blog by Morgan Guyton, "Why does God make eunuchs?" May 21, 2012. Used by permission

of the church movement to restore the "traditional" gender roles of the 19th century family.

To be honest, I don't know if or why God creates people who fall outside of gender normality or if it is simply a product of the fall, which I tend to believe. But I do sense from other stories in the Bible that God actively resists our tendency to moralize normality. When we try to say it's a sin for someone to be born with hormones or organs that are not "normal", and if we are honest with ourselves, that's what we're doing. The problem with moralizing normality is not only that it results in the persecution of those who are born different, but it cheapens morality as well since what we're usually doing is designing our moral system around the purpose of validating our own default "normal" behavior. After all, we all want to think of ourselves as "normal". Perhaps God puts people in our lives who fall outside the norms of identity to force us to refine our moral imagination.

Whatever the case might be, I don't think that transgender identity can be reduced to a social fad. There are undoubtedly people (teachers and parents) who insist on raising children in a "post-gender" kind of way. I'm not comfortable with that because that seems to go beyond accepting those who fall outside the norm and demanding that everyone accept those differences as an ideal. If, on the other hand, you have a boy who can't imagine being anything other than a boy, isn't it going to mess him up to try and make him into a female just as badly as if he were hormonally female and you tried to beat him into being manly? The bottom line is we don't know where other people are coming from or what's going on inside their bodies. What we do know is that if we take Jesus at His word that "there are eunuchs who were born that way" (Matthew 19:12).

And then Jesus also identified as acceptable those *who choose to live like eunuchs* for the sake of the kingdom of heaven" (Matthew 19:12). People who discipline themselves and have no need of sexual fulfillment in their lives can live a celibate lifestyle. Paul lived this way and he indicated that he thought it was a legitimate way to live. "But I say to the unmarried and to the widows: It is good for them if they remain even as I am; but if they cannot exercise self-control, let them marry. For it is better to marry than to burn with passion" (1 Corinthians 7:8–9). It is important to notice however, that his emphasis is on sexual purity, not whether one is married or not.

Listen to what the Lord says concerning the one who is different, but still loves the Lord;

Thus says the Lord:

> "Keep justice, and do righteousness, For My salvation is about to come, And My righteousness to be revealed. Blessed is the man who does this, And the son of man who lays hold on it; Who keeps from defiling the Sabbath and keeps his hand from doing any evil."

> Do not let the son of the foreigner who has joined himself to the Lord speak, saying, "The Lord has utterly separated me from His people"; Nor let the eunuch say, "Here I am, a dry tree." For thus says the Lord: "To the eunuchs who keep My Sabbaths, And choose what pleases Me, and hold fast My covenant, even to them I will give in My house and within My walls a place and a name better than that of sons and daughters; I will give them an everlasting name that shall not be cut off.

> "Also the sons of the foreigner who join themselves to the Lord, to serve Him, and to love the name of the Lord, to be His servants — Everyone who keeps from defiling the Sabbath, and holds fast My covenant — Even them I will bring to My holy mountain, and make them joyful in My house of prayer. Their burnt offerings and their sacrifices will be accepted on My altar; For My house shall be called a house of prayer for all nations." 8 The Lord God, who gathers the outcasts of Israel, says, "Yet I will gather to him others besides those who are gathered to him." (Isaiah 56:1–8)

Notice if you will, the requirement is on God's moral standard, not on how you were born and/or wired.

I must admit that I have chosen to reference another's viewpoint on this particular matter because it is an issue that I have had to personally struggle with. I have two grandchildren, one boy and one girl, who see themselves as the opposite sex. Consequently, I have had to examine my own belief on the subject, and I believe that this particular viewpoint comes about as close to my conclusions as I have run across.[10]

---

[10] The preceding discussion follows closely to the argument Why does God make eunuchs? (Matthew 19:12) | Morgan Guyton (patheos.com) accessed May 5, 2021 (used by permission)

4

THE MINISTRY OF DELIVERANCE

INTRODUCTION

A*lthough raised in* the church and attended church run school for the first 9 grades, I was confronted by the reality of the existence and activity of the demonic in the early 1970's when my wife, who has since died, began exhibiting some strange behaviors. And a respected pastor friend of mine came to me privately and told me that he discerned that she needed spiritual deliverance. I respected him and had experienced his fruitful ministry, so I agreed to cooperate with him in delivering her. At that time, she was not a Christian and I was attempting to pastor a small church in Montana and she was openly resisting the ministry.

During this period, I had planted a church in Montana and we were fellowshipping with another group in Coos Bay, Oregon and had traveled from Montana to Oregon for a visit because our mutual friend was ministering there. On one Saturday evening, when we were having a prayer meeting, my wife reacted rather forcefully during the meeting, which provided opportunity to confront the spirit working in her. I had never participated in an exorcism before, so I was rather surprised at what happened, but to make a long story short, she was delivered and within a year became a Christian. It did awaken an awareness however, that Paul was right when he said "we do not wrestle against flesh and blood, but against principalities, against powers, against the rulers of the darkness of this age, against spiritual hosts of wickedness in the heavenly places" (Ephesians 6:12). That is as true in the 21st century as it was in the 1st century when Paul said it. Therefore, the church needs to be prepared to minister to those who need spiritual deliverance, but to do so with compassion, knowledge and wisdom.

The Ministry of Deliverance is one of the vital ministries of the Church, and, like all other ministries, it is the LORD who calls, equips and anoints the one ministering. It is not a special ministry, nor a higher ministry compared to other ministries of the church. However, it is an important ministry, and not to be entered into lightly. It requires commitment and dedication. Although I had read the Bible and recognized that demons are real and Jesus took them seriously, I bought into the popular point of view that deliverance from demons was an ancient practice and was not needed in the modern era. Similar to the modern view by many Christians that the gifts of the Spirit are no longer needed.

It is important to note that this is one of the first ministries Jesus gave His disciples, as well as one of the main activities Jesus Himself engaged in. He taught a lot, but His ministry always grew out of Him healing the sick and casting demons out of the oppressed. Consider Jesus's choosing of His twelve disciples and what He commissioned them to do as recorded by Mark. "And He went up on the mountain and called to Him those He Himself wanted. And they came to Him. Then He appointed twelve, that they might be with Him and that He might send them out to preach, and to have power to heal sicknesses and to cast out demons" (Mark 3:13–15). Consequently, from a clear account in Scripture, from personal experience, and knowing that Jesus is the same yesterday, today and forever, I believe we have to conclude that there are still demons working under the direct leadership of Satan, and we need to stand firm against them. Listen to Paul's admonition, "Therefore take up the whole armor of God, that you may be able to withstand in the evil day, and having done all, to stand" (Ephesians 6:13).

It would seem the biggest deterrent today to recognizing or naming it as demonic oppression, is the modern tendency to label every "out of the ordinary" behavior as some medical or mental disorder for which the doctor simply needs to prescribe some medicine or counseling therapy.

When a person is willing to admit that the Bible is our best guide for life, God and the Holy Spirit are alive and active in the church as well as the lives of individuals, then we are on our way to discovering the truth about spiritual warfare. That is what the Bible calls spiritual warfare. In fact, Paul, when he was encouraging his disciple Timothy said "(y)ou therefore must endure hardship as a good soldier of Jesus Christ" (2 Timothy 2:3). This is why Scripture tells us to put on the "whole armor of God" (Ephesians 6:13). Further, one of the gifts of the Spirit given to the church for the benefit of all was the "discerning of spirits" (1 Corinthians 12:10b).

There are three specific and very different "spirits" that are present in the world and we need desperately to discern which is speaking, acting, or manifesting themselves at any given time. First if the human spirit. God has given us all soul, that is breath life that gives us mind, will and emotions. God intended for His human creation to have dominion of His creation; therefore, He gave them a powerful mind. In fact, He instructed us to worship Him with our mind. Consequently, human wisdom is powerful and creative, but it is also fallen and perverted, capable of doing immense good or gross evil. Therefore, we need the spiritual ability to discern when someone comes up with an idea, a plan, or a "word" from God, whether it is simply from them and human wisdom, which might be good or bad.

All the ways of a man are pure in his own eyes,

But the Lord weighs the spirits (Proverbs 16:2).

There is also the evil spirit, known as the devil and his hordes of demons.

And no wonder! For Satan himself transforms himself into an angel of light. Therefore it is no great thing if his ministers also transform themselves into ministers of righteousness, whose end will be according to their works (2 Corinthians 11:14–15).

And of course, there is also the Holy Spirit. Consequently, it is imperative that we be able to discern which spirit is speaking, moving or manifesting themselves at any given moment. Our human spirit is capable of speaking out of love, out of anger, out of revenge, or out of the influence of a demon at any given time, so the church needs a way of discerning which it is. As wise as the human is capable of, it is still counted as mere foolishness when compared to God's wisdom. Satan loves to come to church and loves to teach a distorted gospel message to draw away as many people as possible. Therefore, we must be able to discern when the devil or his demons have infiltrated the church attempting to insert some false doctrine or some false hope as Jesus warned us. "Beware of false prophets, who come to you in sheep's clothing, but inwardly they are ravenous wolves" (Matthew 7:15). Peter warned the early church of this danger as well.

> But there were also false prophets among the people, even as there will be false teachers among you, who will secretly bring in destructive heresies, even denying the Lord who bought them, and bring on themselves swift destruction. And many will follow their destructive ways, because of whom the way of truth will be blasphemed (2 Peter 2:1–2)

And the Apostle Paul warned us about this same danger in his letter to the Galatians. "And this occurred because of false brethren secretly brought in (who came in by stealth to spy out our liberty which we have in Christ Jesus, that they might bring us into bondage)" (Galatians 2:4).

My prayer is that the reader can clearly see the need for a deliverance ministry in the church today. It will be present if the leadership of the church will teach the gifts of the Spirit accurately and give way for the manifestation of the Spirit to move freely in the church body.

Now I want to walk through what I believe is an accurate biblical approach to seeing the gift of the discerning of Spirits to be taught and practiced in the church. This was taught as a regular course in the Bible

School my wife and I developed in the Philippines, and I pray it becomes a regular practice in your church as well.

I need to give credit where credit is due as I begin this discussion. Most of the material, ideas and structure for this topic originated from one of our main teachers that teach in the Streams of Living Waters Bible School in the Philippines, Matias Payla. He joined the Bible School as a student in 2011 and not only graduated, but he interpreted for me as I taught at the Talakag site for many years until he took over the ministry in that area in 2015. He has since graduated more students than any other single teaching site. As well, because of the location where he ministered from, he taught at and was in close contact with many remote native villages up in the mountains of that region of Mindanao where native superstition and local pagan worship rituals and practices are an integral part of everyday life. Because of this exposure and experience, he began to develop a curriculum based on biblical principal and practice and he was able to set many people free and bring them into the Kingdom. Over several years we developed this curriculum and finally incorporated it into the degree program of Streams of Living Waters Bible School as a required course. I will use liberally from this curriculum he used in teaching others this vital ministry as well as a few insights I have learned as well. However, we need to understand that the need for deliverance is not limited to the remote native villages of the Philippines. Those oppressed by Satan and his demons walk the streets and attend the church in almost every area of the world, including in the United States of America. Anywhere the body of Christ gathers together, Satan will be present to harass, tempt, and deceive the people.

HOW SATAN WORKS IN AN INDIVIDUAL

We need to discover how these deceiving spirits work and above all to be knowledgeable of how they enter in the first place. There are a multitude of ways that a demon can get a foothold into a person's life. Let's start by looking at some council Paul gave Timothy regarding placing a person in a place of leadership. He said a person should "not (be) a novice, lest being puffed up with pride he fall into the same condemnation as the devil. Moreover he must have a good testimony among those who are outside, lest he fall into reproach and the snare of the devil" (1 Timothy 3:6–7). In other words, the downfall of Satan was pride, and it will open the door of a person's heart to demonic activity if they get lifted up with pride thinking that they are more important than they really are. Notice the downfall of Lucifer, also known as Satan, and what his heart's condition was, because Paul asserts that the same attitude will invade the attitude of a human puffed up with pride.

> How you are fallen from heaven,
> O Lucifer, son of the morning!
> How you are cut down to the ground,
> You who weakened the nations!
> For you have said in your heart:
> 'I will ascend into heaven,
> I will exalt my throne above the stars of God;
> I will also sit on the mount of the congregation
> On the farthest sides of the north;
> I will ascend above the heights of the clouds,
> I will be like the Most High.'
> Yet you shall be brought down to Sheol,
> To the lowest depths of the Pit. (Isaiah 14:12–15)

So it becomes clear that a person's attitude is important and a wrong attitude can lead to demonic activity in their life.

Notice a clear example of how the devil works to bring to the surface human pride. When Jesus was in the wilderness being tempted by the devil for forty days, one of the three temptations was to his pride. As well, notice how Jesus equates pride with worship.

> Again, the devil took Him up on an exceedingly high mountain, and showed Him all the kingdoms of the world and their glory. And he said to Him, "All these things I will give You if You will fall down and worship me."

> Then Jesus said to him, "Away with you, Satan! For it is written, 'You shall worship the Lord your God, and Him only you shall serve.'" (Mattthew 4:8–10)

In talking about how to identify a true teacher from a false teacher Jesus said there is a simple test.

> Beware of false prophets, who come to you in sheep's clothing, but inwardly they are ravenous wolves. You will know them by their fruits. Do men gather grapes from thornbushes or figs from thistles? Even so, every good tree bears good fruit, but a bad tree bears bad fruit. A good tree cannot bear bad fruit, nor can a bad tree bear good fruit. Every tree that does not bear good fruit is cut down and thrown into the fire. Therefore by their fruits you will know them (Matthew 7:15–20).

The point is that when you see a person walking in pride, you will know that they have opened themselves up to the work of the devil in their life and therefore will produce the fruit of demons. The only hope is deliverance from Satan's snare as James advises such a person to "(t)herefore submit to God. Resist the devil and he will flee from you" (James 4:7).

I trust the reader can clearly see that one's attitude is vital to recognize and control as a born-again Christian. It can invite demonic activity or repel it. While there is a debate as to whether a truly born-again Christian can be possessed by a demon, it is without question that anyone, Christian or unbeliever, can be oppressed by a demon. And oppression is the largest threat to Christians today. And while there are various stages and degrees of oppression, this is the condition that requires deliverance. I will offer a thought-provoking list of things the devil uses to oppress God's people with, but this is only a suggestive list and not an exhaustive list. And you might see things on this list that you might not count as oppressive, but the reality is that Satan will use anything that he can convince you is worthy of worship, that is worth giving your life for. And I am not referring to only physically dying for, but giving your time, your talents, your energy, your money, or anything you give in exchange for a vital intimate relationship with Jesus Christ. Oppression affects almost every area of our being – our attitudes, our emotions, our mind or thoughts, and of course our physical body as well.

As I present this rather elaborate list, I feel the need to explain my understanding of Scripture as it pertains to our spiritual warfare. Remember that Jesus was tempted, and Scripture is very clear that He was tempted by the devil (see Matthew 4:1; Mark 1:13; Luke 4:2). Being tempted is a form of oppression and that is the sense that I offer this list of things Satan attempts to tempt us with, which, as I stated, I see as a form of oppression. Listen to James explain this truth in his letter.

> Let no one say when he is tempted, "I am tempted by God"; for God cannot be tempted by evil, nor does He Himself tempt anyone. But each one is tempted when he is drawn away by his own desires and enticed (James 1:13–14).

Consequently, as you read and consider this list, don't assume that you are guilty of sin, but are being tempted by things you might be vulnerable to, and need to be on guard lest the devil take advantage of you.[11]

- **ATTITUDES**

MADNESS	CRAFTY	UNBELIEF	FEAR	TIMIDITY
ARROGANCE	ACTING	INFIRMITIES	MOCKERY	FOOLISHNESS
CUNNING	SHOW-OFF	DOUBT	EXTRAVAGANCE	
ANXIETY	LAZINESS	APATHY	WORRY	

- **EMOTIONS**

INFERIORITY	ANGER	HATRED	CONCEIT	RESENTMENT
LONELINESS	REJECTION	UNLOVED	UNWANTED	SUPERIORITY

---

[11] This list was agreed upon by the teachers of Streams of Living Waters Bible School, Inc. Tagoloan, Philippines and is not knowingly taken from any published material.

- **MIND/THOUGHTS**

MADNESS	CONFUSIONS	SILLINESS	STUPIDITY	DULL
TELEPATHY	CONCENTRATION	EMPTINESS	VOID	SUICIDE
TELEKENISIS	MENTAL	BLOCK		

- **PHYSICAL**

LUST	GLUTTONY	PAIN	TIRENESS	ANEMIA
ADULTERY	FORNICATION	OBSCENITY	CHOKING	CANCER
ADDICTION	UNCLEAN	DEFORMATION	ALLERGIES	NAUSEA
PERVERSION	MASTURBATION	ARTHRITIS	NERVES	SICKNESS
INFIRMITIES	INSOMIA			

These are all things that lead to oppression, but there is such a thing as demon possession as well. This is where a demon actually moves into the body of an individual and takes over total control of that person. We see several examples of this in Scripture and Jesus had to cast them out in Mark's gospel.

> Then they came to the other side of the sea, to the country of the Gadarenes. And when He had come out of the boat, immediately there met Him out of the tombs a man with an unclean spirit, who had his dwelling among the tombs; and no one could bind him, not even with chains, because he had often been bound with shackles and chains. And the chains had been pulled apart by him, and the shackles broken in pieces; neither could anyone tame him. And always, night and day, he was in the mountains and in the tombs, crying out and cutting himself with stones.
>
> When he saw Jesus from afar, he ran and worshiped Him. And he cried out with a loud voice and said, "What have I to do with You, Jesus, Son of the Most High God? I implore You by God that You do not torment me."

For He said to him, "Come out of the man, unclean spirit!" Then He asked him, "What is your name?"

And he answered, saying, "My name is Legion; for we are many." Also he begged Him earnestly that He would not send them out of the country (Mark 5:1–10).

Notice that the man had no control over his actions but was totally controlled by the demon spirits that possessed him. He could not even really speak for himself, because Jesus had to speak directly to the demons and command that they leave. This is the main difference between oppression and possession. When you are oppressed, you still have some control over your behavior and usually can be reasoned with, whereas someone who is possessed is not in control of their own behaviors and must be dealt with in a different manner. Some of the symptoms of a possessed person are that they might display extraordinary activities, demonstrate super strength, show extraordinary knowledge, or powers, and in almost all cases will show a demonstrable change of personality, and in some cases will show no sign of consciousness.

CAUSES OF DEMON POSSESSION

Satan or Demon Worship

What are the causes for demon possession? Paul is instructive as we listen to him teach his young disciple Timothy how to disciple others, especially leaders.

But avoid foolish and ignorant disputes, knowing that they generate strife. And a servant of the Lord must not quarrel but be gentle to all, able to teach, patient, in humility correcting those who are in opposition, if God perhaps will grant them repentance, so that they may know the truth, and that they may come to their senses and escape the snare of the devil, having been taken captive by him to do his will (2 Timothy 2:23–26).

Notice that he mentions "those who are in opposition" to what God is saying, which means that they are actively working against the gospel message. And the result is that as they oppose God, they are "taken captive by him (the devil) to do his will" rather than doing God's will. Notice as well that this one who is opposing God is "taken captive". Of course, one who is taken captive, is not free anymore to do what he/she wants but is subject to the one who has taken them captive. Think of someone who had been arrested and taken to jail. That person is not free to do as they please any longer but has to submit to jail law.

Paul gets very specific about how a person can come under the influence of demons when he is discussing the question of how believers are to interact with non-believers in his letter to the Corinthians who are struggling in their relationship with non-believer friends and family.

Observe Israel after the flesh: Are not those who eat of the sacrifices partakers of the altar? What am I saying then? That an idol is anything, or what is offered to idols is anything? Rather, that the things which the Gentiles sacrifice they sacrifice to demons and not to God, and I do not want you to have fellowship with demons. You cannot drink the cup of the Lord and the cup of demons; you cannot partake of the Lord's table and of the table of demons. Or do we provoke the Lord to jealousy? Are we stronger than He? (1 Corinthians 10:18–22)

He illustrates his point by referring to the Jews own law and their sacrifices. The pagans also had a rather elaborate religious tradition of sacrifices to their gods, including in many instances, sacrificing their own children. The point is that in partaking of religious rituals that include demonic activity, they are directly participating with the demon, just like when they offer a sacrifice for their sins to the priest, they know that they are directly interacting with their God, as their God is a jealous God who surely notices when they are flirting with another god. Therefore, he wants them to understand that along with the act of worship that they are engaging in with their friend or relative, they are opening themselves to the activity of a demon in their own life. Of course, today most people don't offer animal sacrifices, but most do engage in rituals to honor the "things" that are of most important in their lives. The point is that these things are truly "gods" and as a Christian engages in things like drunken parties, drug use that altars the mind, as well as other seemingly harmless activities, they open up their minds to demonic activity. God is still a jealous God today and will react to that behavior in some way. Listen to how Moses described God's attitude toward those who would entertain demons.

> They provoked Him to jealousy with foreign gods;
> With abominations they provoked Him to anger.
> They sacrificed to demons, not to God,
> To gods they did not know,
> To new gods, new arrivals
> That your fathers did not fear.
> Of the Rock who begot you, you are unmindful,
> And have forgotten the God who fathered you.
> (Deuteronomy 32:16–18)

See also Exodus 20:5–6 and Psalm 106:36–38 for further descriptions of God's attitude toward His people allowing demonic activity into their lives.

While there is such a thing as demonic possession, as I said earlier, most of the demonic activity comes when we deliberately open our minds and lives up to it. When this happens, we still for the most part, need outside help to be delivered from the consequences. This is where one who has been given the ministry of deliverance is needed.

Dedication of Children To Demons or Other Gods

Another way that a demon can enter a person's life is by the parent's actions when the children are young. Many people and cultures have some ceremony of dedicating their children when they are born or still incredibly young. And not all those ceremonies of dedication are good. In fact, many rituals are actually of the devil and can lead to demonic activity in the child's life as they are growing up, and even into adulthood. Of course, most evangelical churches that do not believe in child baptism, will have some type of ceremony, usually public, where they "dedicate" their child to God. For the most part when done in the Name of the Lord, are good and appropriate, and are meant more as a reminder to parents of the biblical charge to raise their children in the fear and admonition of the Lord (Ephesians 6:4). Nevertheless, there are many examples of such dedications that are dangerous and open up both child and parent to demonic activity. For example, there is a folk ritual in the Philippines called "Padugo" where an animal is sacrificed through a blood spilling ritual that is thought to give good luck to the child as he/she grows up. This is a superstitious ritual similar to many other superstitions that many people follow trying to gain the favor of "god" which the Bible tells us is nothing but demonic. Superstitious rituals include the phrase "knock on wood", crossing one's fingers, and I remember a rather subtle one that my first father-in-law used to do. There was a superstition that he was exposed to as a child which he practiced to the day of his death. He loved to play pinocle (a card game) and whenever he was having "bad luck" in his draw of cards, he would get out of his chair and walk around the chair three times, believing that this practice would change his luck and now he would have "good luck" in his card draws. Any such superstitious behavior is offensive to God. He warns us that participating in such activities will open up our mind to demonic activity, which will only lead to more and more oppression until we are delivered from it.

Another practice that opens a person to demonic activity is the wearing of tokens or amulets that are small ornaments thought to give protection from demonic activity, but only enhances the probability. This is actually another form of superstition, but is some ornament with some symbolic meaning, either just for the person, but often a cultural symbol that has meaning to a group of people. I have seen Christians wear a cross as a necklace thinking that somehow they were influencing God to give them special protection. Any symbol, even religious symbols when thought to have some mystical power to protect, influence, or have some innate power of their own, are an abomination to God and can open up your mind to demonic influence and activity.

Another deceptive activity people engage in regularly is the giving of some vow in exchange for some favor or to receive a "good life". Listen to Solomon speak of the vow –

> When you make a vow to God, do not delay to pay it;
>
> For He has no pleasure in fools.
>
> Pay what you have vowed —
>
> Better not to vow than to vow and not pay.
>
> Do not let your mouth cause your flesh to sin, nor say before the messenger of God that it was an error. Why should God be angry at your excuse and destroy the work of your hands? For in the multitude of dreams and many words there is also vanity. But fear God. (Ecclesiastes 5:4–7)

In fact, because this was such a big problem in Jesus's day He addressed it directly and pointedly.

> Again you have heard that it was said to those of old, 'You shall not swear falsely, but shall perform your oaths to the Lord.' But I say to you, do not swear at all: neither by heaven, for it is God's throne; nor by the earth, for it is His footstool; nor by Jerusalem, for it is the city of the great King. Nor shall you swear by your head, because you cannot make one hair white or black. But let your

'Yes' be 'Yes,' and your 'No,' 'No.' For whatever is more
than these is from the evil one. (Matthew 5:33–37)

And I pray that we can see the purpose of restraining from making vows. We don't know what today holds for us, let alone tomorrow or next week, and absolutely not next year. Engaging in such behavior opens a person's mind to the influence of the "evil one", and the evil one will not be kind to you, bring you a good life, or bring you good luck. He has only one purpose and that is to lie, cheat, and steal from you. We need to understand the Scriptural teaching about Satan clearly. He is the one who comes and steals the Word of God out of the heart of the young and weak (Luke 8:12). And he is the one who tempts people with evil (Matthew 4:1), takes people captive (2 Timothy 2:26), deceives the whole world (Revelation 12:9), and even has some people thrown into prison (Revelation 2:10). However, he is not to be feared, but he is to be actively resisted (James 4:7). Jesus taught His disciples an important lesson when He taught them about the difference between a good shepherd and a fake shepherd, interested only in his own benefit. Notice that Jesus equates the "thief" as Satan as He warns that "(t)he thief does not come except to steal, and to kill, and to destroy. I have come that they may have life, and that they may have it more abundantly" (John 10:10).

One last practice I want to mention and that is the practice of many parents who engage their children in some of their own addictions and oppressions at home. For example, how many parents openly use foul language in the home around their young children. And the children grow up using language that they really don't even understand, and it can lead to demonic activity in the child's life as they grow up. Or how about parent's who use drugs or alcohol regularly in the home around their children. The children learn early that those habits are okay, even good, therefore, some will grow up thinking that using drugs or alcohol is good and can allow demonic activity when under the influence of drugs or alcohol for some. This is why Moses instructed families to fill family time with speaking about God and His goodness and the benefits of serving and worshipping Him (Deuteronomy 6: 1–6). And we can't neglect the teaching of Paul, "(a)nd you, fathers, do not provoke your children to wrath, but bring them up in the training and admonition of the Lord" (Ephesians 6:4). It is mandatory for us parents to know and live in God's Word and to teach them diligently to our children. Otherwise, we open them up to the deception of the devil and his hoard of demons "walks about like a roaring lion, seeking whom he may devour" (1 Peter 5:8b).

Witchcraft, Occultism, and Spiritism

Another way that people are exposed to demonic oppression or possession is through the ancient practice of witchcraft, occultism or spiritism, all of which are openly practiced in most parts of the world still today. While there are many examples, I want to begin by discussing what Scripture has to say on the subject. After all, that should be our guide for lifestyle and behavior. I want to show God's strict command not to engage these evil spirits in the first place. "Give no regard to mediums and familiar spirits; do not seek after them, to be defiled by them: I am the Lord your God" (Leviticus 19:31). And he gets even more specific in Leviticus 20: 6–7.

And the person who turns to mediums and familiar spirits, to prostitute himself with them, I will set My face against that person and cut him off from his people. Consecrate yourselves therefore, and be holy, for I am the Lord your God. 8 And you shall keep My statutes, and perform them: I am the Lord who sanctifies you.

And as Moses was instructing the Nation of Israel on their behavior just before entering the Promised Land, his warning against such behavior was clear and specific.

> When you come into the land which the Lord your
> God is giving you, you shall not learn to follow the
> abominations of those nations. There shall not be found
> among you anyone who makes his son or his daughter
> pass through the fire, or one who practices witchcraft, or
> a soothsayer, or one who interprets omens, or a sorcerer,
> or one who conjures spells, or a medium, or a spiritist, or
> one who calls up the dead. For all who do these things

are an abomination to the Lord, and because of these abominations the Lord your God drives them out from before you. You shall be blameless before the Lord your God. For these nations which you will dispossess listened to soothsayers and diviners; but as for you, the Lord your God has not appointed such for you. (Deuteronomy 18:9–14)

Some practices that we see in various cultures around the world, including right here in the United States of America include the following.[12]

HORROSCOPE	ASTROLOGY	PALMISTRY	KARATE
FOTUNE TELLING	SPIRITISM	FRATERNITY	CARD READING
CONCENTRATION	SPIRIT OF THE GLASS	PSYCHIC EXPERIENCE	
DEEP BREATHING	GLASS		

I feel the need to explain some of these since not everyone has been exposed to them, or maybe exposed by another name and ignorant of the real meaning or danger of the practice. And I know as well that not everyone will agree with everything listed here. The sad fact is that many of these practices have been introduced to a culture under the guise of some "good" thing that will bring the user some benefit. For example, karate has infiltrated many cultures as a legitimate form of self defense and good for physical exercise. The fact of the matter is, nevertheless, that karate is a form of many eastern, mainly Asian cultures as a religious exercise meant to program the mind in a certain way to control your thoughts and reactions to outside stimuli. It can open one's mind to further spiritual activity, which is demonic at its core. Christians are to "be renewed in the spirit of your mind" (Ephesians 4:23). And the next verse explains why, "and that you put on the new man which was created according to God, in true righteousness and holiness" (Ephesians 4:24).

---

[12] Again, this list was agreed upon by the teachers of Streams of Living Waters Bible School, Inc. Tagoloan, Philippines and not knowingly from any published list.

So, anything that programs the mind or will in any way outside of God's Word and will is demonic and should be avoided by Christians.

Another one that might not be familiar to some is "spirit of the glass" or as some simply refer to it as "glass". Spirit of the glass refers to a number of games that are meant to summon spirits in order to attempt to give needed information, or prevent certain events, or at least change the course of events to predict the outcome. One of the better known versions of this practice is the Ouija board. Many people have been deceived by such practices, thinking that they were summoning the spirits of friends or loved ones, when in actuality what they experienced was evil spirits, and in doing so provided an opening for demonic activity in their life or the life of their family through seemingly innocent games. I am personally aware of a sobering experience at a boarding school in Montana where some students gathered together and played with a Ouija board and in the process one of the main buildings on the campus was burned down. Parents especially need to be aware of the games their children play, because there are a growing number of games designed to open up children's minds to the occult. As noted earlier, we as Christians are called to be sober and vigilant in our walk with the Lord, "because your adversary the devil walks about like a roaring lion, seeking whom he may devour. Resist him, steadfast in the faith, knowing that the same sufferings are experienced by your brotherhood in the world" (1 Peter 5:8b–9).

Soul-Ties

Soul-ties is still another way that people open themselves up to demonic activity. This one is a little harder to define but the term simply refers to the soul of an individual that becomes tied to another person's soul. The confusing part is that it is actually a biblical principle although the term itself is never used in Scripture. A biblical example is found in the marriage bond.

> So husbands ought to love their own wives as their own
> bodies; he who loves his wife loves himself. For no one

ever hated his own flesh, but nourishes and cherishes it, just as the Lord does the church. For we are members of His body, of His flesh and of His bones. "For this reason a man shall leave his father and mother and be joined to his wife, and the two shall become one flesh." (Ephesians 5:28–31)

And it becomes clear that this soul-tie between a husband and wife is not to be broken.

But from the beginning of the creation, God 'made them male and female.' 'For this reason a man shall leave his father and mother and be joined to his wife, and the two shall become one flesh'; so then they are no longer two, but one flesh. Therefore what God has joined together, let not man separate." (Mark 10:6–9)

So that is how God intended our human relationships to be, especially the marriage relationship. However, there is another biblical example of acceptable soul-ties, and that is David and Jonathan who developed a soul-tie relationship. "Now when he had finished speaking to Saul, the soul of Jonathan was knit to the soul of David, and Jonathan loved him as his own soul" (1 Samuel 18:1–2).

Nevertheless, the Bible also gives an example of an unholy soul-tie that can be dangerous and lead to demonic influence and frankly, one that still plagues most cultures today, and that is an unhealthy sexual relationship. A sexual relationship develops a bond between the individuals involved and when it is outside of God's design for a sexual relationship, it can leave the door open for demonic activity. Listen to Paul explain this dangerous soul-tie relationship.

Do you not know that your bodies are members of Christ? Shall I then take the members of Christ and make them members of a harlot? Certainly not! Or do you not know that he who is joined to a harlot is one body with her? For "the two," He says, "shall become one flesh." But he who is joined to the Lord is one spirit with Him.

Flee sexual immorality. Every sin that a man does is outside the body, but he who commits sexual immorality sins against his own body. Or do you not know that your body is the temple of the Holy Spirit who is in you, whom you have from God, and you are not your own? For you were bought at a price; therefore glorify God in your body and in your spirit, which are God's. (1 Corinthians 6:15–20)

I have known women, and it can and does happen to men also, where she becomes involved in a marriage or an affair with a man who becomes abusive, and because her soul is tied closely to his, as well as the bond of their sexual relationship, when the relationship breaks up, she will end up finding another man with the same abusive characteristics because her soul is tied to that behavior. It is also very common for people who make a vow to another to have their souls tied together. Of course, when a couple gets married they do and should make vows to each other, but when a person makes a vow of friendship, or some vow of commitment, it is possible for their souls to be tied together. That is one of the many reasons Scripture says that it is better to not make a vow than to make a vow and not to keep it (Ecclesiastes 5:5). The problem arises when a person ties their soul to the wrong person, or under the wrong circumstances, it can be very harmful, and the result is that you leave your soul open for demonic activity and influence. Another person can literally control another person through the soul tie, and the person is not even aware that they are being controlled. This can even be done legally when you make a legal contract, such as a business contract, or even a business partnership with another that ties you closely together.

Scripture is clear that God is concerned that we take care of our souls and be very careful who we create a bond with. Parents need to understand this truth and teach their children to choose their friends very carefully. And we all need to understand this truth when we are dating and choosing a mate. A mate can either make you or break you, or, in too many cases, put you at the devil's mercy, and he has no mercy. As mentioned above, even going into business with an unbeliever can put you in the bondage of a soul-tie. If you find yourself influenced in a soul tie with the wrong person, you will need to deliberately break that tie. Many times it will require the help of a person who is experienced in deliverance ministry. Just like Jesus spent an incredible amount of His ministry casting out demons and setting the oppressed free, there are ministries today that can do the same thing.

Direct Disobedience to Divine Principles

Like some of the other ways a person can come under oppression of the devil are controversial, this one is no exception. Nevertheless, direct disobedience to known Divine principles will certainly open a person up to demonic activity and oppression, and in some cases, possession. But we need to recognize that Satan is a liar and the father of lies.

> You are of your father the devil, and the desires of your father you want to do. He was a murderer from the beginning, and does not stand in the truth, because there is no truth in him. When he speaks a lie, he speaks from his own resources, for he is a liar and the father of it. (John 8:44)

Remember Satan is not only a liar and a deceiver, but he also works in the dark, and darkness does not like light. So, we need to come into the light, so the works of darkness are exposed. "In Him was life, and the life was the light of men. And the light shines in the darkness, and the darkness did not comprehend it" (John 1:4–5).

Idolatry

The first way I want to discuss concerning direct disobedience to Divine principles is the all-too often practiced idolatry. I preached a sermon a few years ago titled *Idols of the Heart*, and in it I spoke of modern-day idols. Most people today would not think of literally bowing down to an idol and praying to it, but we still set up idols in our heart. And that is no different in God's eyes than having a physical idol made from metal, wood, ceramic, or today, even plastic. God warned Israel centuries ago about having idols, whether physically or spiritually.

> You shall not make for yourself a carved image — any
> likeness of anything that is in heaven above, or that is in
> the earth beneath, or that is in the water under the earth;
> you shall not bow down to them nor serve them. For I,
> the Lord your God, am a jealous God (Exodus 20:4-5a).

And Moses reminded the people of this command just as they were ready to enter the Promised Land and encounter the many idols the inhabitants of the land worshiped. And then many years later when Israel had come under the severe judgment of God for neglecting this command and having many idols they worshipped, the prophet Jeremiah had this to say about God's attitude toward a people who would turn to an idol rather than their living God.

> Now therefore, thus says the Lord, the God of hosts, the
> God of Israel: 'Why do you commit this great evil against
> yourselves, to cut off from you man and woman, child
> and infant, out of Judah, leaving none to remain, in that
> you provoke Me to wrath with the works of your hands,
> burning incense to other gods in the land of Egypt where
> you have gone to dwell, that you may cut yourselves off
> and be a curse and a reproach among all the nations of the
> earth? Have you forgotten the wickedness of your fathers,
> the wickedness of the kings of Judah, the wickedness of
> their wives, your own wickedness, and the wickedness of
> your wives, which they committed in the land of Judah
> and in the streets of Jerusalem? They have not been

humbled, to this day, nor have they feared; they have not walked in My law or in My statutes that I set before you and your fathers.' (Jeremiah 44:7–10)

The fact of the matter is that this was not the only time in the church's history that idolatry was a problem. John Calvin famously said, "the human heart is a perpetual idol factory".[13] It was a problem in Noah's day, it was a problem in Abraham's day, it was a problem in Moses's day, it was a problem during the entire history of the nation of Israel, and it is still a problem today. The only difference is that today people carry their idols in their hearts and minds, but it is still offensive to God.

Christian leaders Tim Keller, David Powlison, Dick Keyes and many others have written extensively on the idols of the heart, but here is a snapshot of four root idols that they conclude drive our behavior. And some of you might recognize that all four of these were included in the temptations that Satan tempted Jesus with during His forty days in the Judean wilderness. First, is the power, that is a longing for influence or recognition. Second is control, which is a longing to have everything go according to "MY" plan, while the third idol is comfort, that longing for pleasure, which manifests itself in entertainment, recreation, sports, sex, drugs, or any other behavior that brings pleasure to oneself. And the fourth idol of the heart is approval, a longing to be accepted or desired.

We need to understand that these things in and of themselves are not evil. Or as Calvin stated, "The evil in our desire typically does not lie in what we want, but that we want it too much."[14] So how do we keep ourselves free as John encourages us? "Little children, keep yourselves from idols" (1 John 5:21). It should be obvious to one who knows Jesus's words to us,

"I am the true vine, and My Father is the vinedresser. Every branch in Me that does not bear fruit He takes away; and every branch that bears fruit He prunes, that it may bear more fruit. You are already clean because of

---

[13] John Calvin, Institutes of the Christian Religion, 1559 Definitive Edition, I.11.8
[14] John Calvin, Institutes of the Christian Religion, 1559 Definitive Edition, I.11.8

the word which I have spoken to you. Abide in Me, and I in you. As the branch cannot bear fruit of itself, unless it abides in the vine, neither can you, unless you abide in Me.

"I am the vine, you are the branches. He who abides in Me, and I in him, bears much fruit; for without Me you can do nothing. If anyone does not abide in Me, he is cast out as a branch and is withered; and they gather them and throw them into the fire, and they are burned. If you abide in Me, and My words abide in you, you will ask what you desire, and it shall be done for you. By this My Father is glorified, that you bear much fruit; so you will be My disciples. (John 15:1–8)

So, as we abide in Him and allow Him to dwell in us through His Holy Spirit, He works on those idols of our heart. I like what Eric Geiger says about combating and winning over those idols that are so persuasive at getting Christians to worship before them. He says that we should repent and recognize the greater God within us. He suggests that we go before God and say, "I repent of my idolatry not by looking myself in the mirror and telling myself I can displace it in my energy, might, or goodness. I repent of my lesser gods by remembering the Great God who is above all gods.[15]

Eric Geiger goes on in the same sermon to suggest ways we can repent of our longing for any one of these root idols that we recognize ourselves worshiping before.[16]

- power by submitting to His greater power within me [Ephesians 5:18]
- control by surrendering to His ultimate control [Ecclesiastes 3:12–14]

---

[15] "FOUR ROOT IDOLS" a sermon preached by Eric Geiger Oct. 1, 2013 accessed on 3/3/2021 at https://ericgeiger.com/2013/10/four-root-idols/
[16] Ibid

- comfort by remembering He is the greater comfort [II Corinthians 1:3–4]
- approval by rejoicing in His gracious approval [Galatians 3:13; Numbers 6:24–26]

Possession of Cursed Objects

The second practice where we engage in direct disobedience to God that can lead to demonic control in an individual is to possess curse objects. Certain objects are forever cursed by God and when we insist on ignoring God's clear command to put them away from us, we open ourselves up to demonic activity. Listen to Moses instruct Israel on this matter as they were getting ready to enter the Promised Land. The issue was that it was obvious that when the people went across the Jorden river into Caanan that they would interact with the inhabitants of the land, and in some cases even make friends or do business with them. Consequently, God was concerned that the people not be attracted to their cultural practice of making and worshipping their gods. Therefore, He instructed them in this way.

> For they will turn your sons away from following Me, to serve other gods; so the anger of the Lord will be aroused against you and destroy you suddenly. But thus you shall deal with them: you shall destroy their altars, and break down their sacred pillars, and cut down their wooden images, and burn their carved images with fire.

You shall burn the carved images of their gods with fire; you shall not covet the silver or gold that is on them, nor take it for yourselves, lest you be snared by it; for it is an abomination to the Lord your God. Nor shall you bring an abomination into your house, lest you be doomed to destruction like it. You shall utterly detest it and utterly abhor it, for it is an accursed thing. (Deuteronomy 7:4–5 & 25–26).

The list of possible "accursed" things is too diverse to list in detail here because that list probably would be slightly different depending on the cultural background of the person or people involved. However, many Christians today are ignorant of the fact that certain objects, movies, songs and even clothes are not only displeasing to God, but that they invite demonic oppression, even sickness into their home. As born-again Christians, we should take great care regarding pictures and objects with which we decorate our homes. Many things, especially from Asian countries where Eastern religions flourish, invoke demonic activity. You might remember a church in the Book of Acts when Paul taught them about the gospel, gathered together all the evil spiritual books that many of the members had and burned them. "Also, many of those who had practiced magic brought their books together and burned them in the sight of all. And they counted up the value of them, and it totaled fifty thousand pieces of silver. So the word of the Lord grew mightily and prevailed" (Acts 19:19–20).

So, it becomes clear that demons can inhabit inanimate objects and we need to be aware, because Satan is the great deceiver, and he would want people ignorant of his devices for deceiving and drawing people under his influence. Paul spoke of this necessity as he was trying to teach the Corinthian church the principle of forgiveness, when he said, "lest Satan should take advantage of us; for we are not ignorant of his devices" (2 Corinthians 2:11). Remember, Satan goes around the world looking for someone that he can deceive and lead into some behavior where he can gain a foothold, and thereby destroy that person. That is what the armor of God is that Paul revealed to us in his letter to the Ephesians.

Robbing God in Tithes and Offerings

Robbing God of our tithes and offerings is the third practice where we engage in direct disobedience to God that can lead to demonic control in an individual. The prophet Malachi spoke directly to this problem.

> You are cursed with a curse,
> For you have robbed Me,
> Even this whole nation. (Malachi 3:9)

Now I am aware that many people today claim that tithing was an Old Testament law, therefore it has nothing to do with the church today. However, those same people are ignorant of the fact that while there was a tithe in the Law of Moses, the offering of a tithe was actually practiced for well over four hundred years before Moses ever gave the law. When Abraham met the Priest of God Most High, the King of Salem, Melchizedek, Abraham gave Melchizedek a tithe of everything he had gained. So, it becomes obvious that somewhere, and it is not recorded precisely where or when, tithing was a principal that God taught his priests well before the law. And it doesn't seem like God had changed His mind. Yes, it is true that when Jesus fulfilled the law on Calvary's cross, the law of Moses was done away with and a new law was instituted, known as the law of love. Nevertheless, tithing is God's way of blessing His people. Listen carefully the remainder of Malachi's words to clearly see why God wants us to tithe.

> Bring all the tithes into the storehouse,
> That there may be food in My house,
> And try Me now in this,"
> Says the Lord of hosts,
> "If I will not open for you the windows of heaven
> And pour out for you such blessing
> That there will not be room enough to receive it.
> And I will rebuke the devourer for your sakes,
> So that he will not destroy the fruit of your ground,
> Nor shall the vine fail to bear fruit for you in the field,"
> Says the Lord of hosts;
> And all nations will call you blessed,
> For you will be a delightful land,"
> Says the Lord of hosts. (Malachi 3:10–12)

Tithing is God's way of providing for His people, much like the farmer who wants an abundant crop will plant his field with an abundance of seed. While I do not embrace the modern version of the "prosperity message" that says that God wants all His children rich, I do embrace the biblical model that God wants to provide abundantly for His people which He has purposed through His eternal law of sowing and reaping. And when we reject God's Word, we reject Him and open up ourselves to demonic influence in our life.

Eating of Blood

Finally, the fourth way we engage in direct disobedience to God that can lead to demonic control in an individual is to eat blood. It is a widespread practice among many cultures, and I have been rebuked on many occasions when speaking to cultures that practice eating or drinking blood. Moses was very clear and specific when he instructed Israel on her behavior.

> Whatever man of the children of Israel, or of the strangers who dwell among you, who hunts and catches any animal or bird that may be eaten, he shall pour out its blood and cover it with dust; for it is the life of all flesh. Its blood sustains its life. Therefore I said to the children of Israel, 'You shall not eat the blood of any flesh, for the life of all flesh is its blood. Whoever eats it shall be cut off.' (Leviticus 17:13–14)

And, once again, some would argue such a taboo is Old Testament and, therefore, not applicable to the church today. And if that were true, I would certainly agree with you. However, one only has to read a short distance into the history of the New Testament church in Luke's book of Acts where we see the first church council address this very issue. There we read the full account of the official decision and decree of this first church council.

Since we have heard that some who went out from us have troubled you with words, unsettling your souls, saying, "You must be circumcised and keep the law" — to whom we gave no such commandment — it seemed good to us, being assembled with one accord, to send chosen men to you with our beloved Barnabas and Paul, men who have risked their lives for the name of our Lord Jesus Christ. We have therefore sent Judas and Silas, who will also report the same things by word of mouth. For it seemed good to the Holy Spirit, and to us, to lay upon you no greater burden than these necessary things: that you abstain from things offered to idols, from blood, from things strangled, and from sexual immorality. If you keep yourselves from these, you will do well. (Acts 15:24–29)

I trust that you noticed that the prohibition included even animals that were strangled to death. This is also a practice by some, and the purpose is to force the blood into the flesh of the animal so as to change the flavor of the meat. I have personally known some who would torment the animal just before slaughtering in order to get the adrenalin flowing in the animal and thereby force a larger blood content into the flesh of the animal, because, again, it would change the flavor of the meat that some believe makes it taste better. Nevertheless, God again is very specific as to why He does not want people to eat the blood of any flesh. Notice carefully the words of Leviticus 17 that were quoted above, "'You shall not eat the blood of any flesh, **for the life of all flesh is its blood**" (emphasis mine). God created both animals and humans and gave both "the breath of life" (Genesis 2:7), therefore, to eat or drink that life is an abomination to God. Of course, there is no wondering why Satan would make this a controversial subject. Anything that is sacred to God is an abomination to Satan and he wants to deceive God's people into defiling everything holy to Him. Blood contains the very life for living creatures, and it was given to them by their Creator, and that Creator has asked humankind to refrain from eating it. To disregard this command is to disregard God. Whenever we purposefully disregard God, we are wide open to demonic influence.

CURSES

A Willful Choice of a Cursed Life

We find the first way to fall under a curse in Deuteronomy 28 where Moses describes the curses that a person, or a whole nation, would bring upon themselves for disobeying the law of God. Again, some would argue that since we are no longer under bondage to the law of Moses, God will not bring curses upon us anymore. However, we should rethink that position because Scripture also teaches that God is the same yesterday, today, and forever. Therefore, while the circumstances might be different because God doesn't require us to obey the law of Moses, He does still require us to obey Him. Paul tried to teach the church in Rome this principal, because it was a common practice in the early New Testament church to believe that since believers are no longer obligated to the law of Moses, that they were then free to do those things prohibited in the law. Three times in the first few chapters of his letter to the Roman church Paul asks a rhetorical question, "(w)hat shall we say then? Shall we continue in sin that grace may abound?" (Romans 6:1). And all three times he answers that question in the same way, "(c)ertainly not! How shall we who died to sin live any longer in it?" (Romans 6:2). In other words, sin is present in the world independent of the law, and God still hates sin and there are consequences for sin. Let me give you just two examples that make it clear there are consequences for deliberate sin and I believe that deliberate sin is still equivalent to falling under the curse and is still leaving oneself open to demonic activity in one's life.

In his first letter to the church at Corinth, Paul became aware of a very sinful practice in the church that he insisted brought curses upon them. The example he gives concerns a practice they developed over what has been named in today's church as communion or the Lord's Supper. The congregation in Corinth was treating it as a public demonstration of one's social or economic status and Paul said that it was sin and brought curses on them in the form of physical illness or even death.

> Therefore whoever eats this bread or drinks this cup of the Lord in an unworthy manner will be guilty of the body and blood of the Lord. But let a man examine himself, and so let him eat of the bread and drink of the cup. For he who eats and drinks in an unworthy manner eats and drinks judgment to himself, not discerning the Lord's body. For this reason many are weak and sick among

you, and many sleep. For if we would judge ourselves, we would not be judged. But when we are judged, we are chastened by the Lord, that we may not be condemned with the world. (1 Corinthians 11:27–32)

Paul gives one more example of the effects of deliberate disobedience to God's commandments and the curse that accompanies it. A man had committed a heinous sin by sleeping with his father's wife, and apparently would not repent of it so Paul describes the consequences of his actions.

In the name of our Lord Jesus Christ, when you are gathered together, along with my spirit, with the power of our Lord Jesus Christ, deliver such a one to Satan for the destruction of the flesh, that his spirit may be saved in the day of the Lord Jesus. (1 Corinthians 5:4–5)

So, understand clearly that falling under a curse for disobedience is not just an Old Testament probability; but it is still probable today when a believer decides to sin willfully, disregarding the commandment of the Lord.

Bringing Curse Upon Oneself and Family

The second way to fall under a curse for yourself or your whole family is in the form of taking oaths. I talked earlier about God's attitude about taking an oath, when Jesus said,

Again you have heard that it was said to those of old, 'You shall not swear falsely, but shall perform your oaths to the Lord.' But I say to you, do not swear at all: neither by heaven, for it is God's throne; nor by the earth, for it is His footstool; nor by Jerusalem, for it is the city of the great King. Nor shall you swear by your head, because you cannot make one hair white or black. But let your

'Yes' be 'Yes,' and your 'No,' 'No.' For whatever is more
than these is from the evil one. (Matthew 5:33–37)

Regardless of this abundantly clear prohibition against oath taking,
many groups through the centuries have insisted upon forcing people
to take an oath in order to become a member of some group or society.
"The Knights Templar were warriors dedicated to protecting Christian
pilgrims to the Holy Land during the Crusades. The military order
was founded around 1118 when Hugues de Payens, a French knight,
created the Poor Fellow-Soldiers of Christ and the Temple of Solomon—
or The Knights Templar for short. Headquartered at Temple Mount
in Jerusalem, members pledged to live a life of chastity, obedience and
poverty, abstaining from gambling, alcohol and even swearing."[17] And
the dangerous thing about these organizations is that they all require
members to swear allegiance to the organization, which of course is
clearly prohibited by Scripture. Swearing an oath and not being able to
keep it puts the person at the mercy of Satan and his curses.

Another example is Freemasonry, a secret society founded formally
in 1717. Although it had its early beginnings as early as 1390, it did not
formally organize as we know it today until 1717 in London. "Freemasonry
is not a religion, though members are encouraged to believe in a <u>Supreme
Being</u>, or "Grand Architect of the Universe." Masonic temples and secret
rituals have brought them into conflict with the Catholic Church. The
Church first condemned the freemasons in 1738 and has gone on to
issue around 20 decrees against them. In 1985, Roman Catholic Bishops
restated over 200 years' worth of these strictures in the face of an increased
number of Catholics joining the order." "The Church wasn't their only
enemy; the secrecy of the masons garnered such distrust in early America
that it inspired America's first "third party": The Anti-Masonic Party."[18]

There are a number of secret societies or fraternities around the
world, especially on many college campuses, and all such societies require

---

[17] History accessed on 3/8/2021 at htpps://www.history.com/news/secret-societies-
freemasons-knights-templar <u>5 of History's Most Mysterious Secret Societies - HISTORY</u>
[18] History accessed on 3/8/2021 at htpps://www.history.com/news/secret-societies-
freemasons-knights-templar <u>5 of History's Most Mysterious Secret Societies - HISTORY</u>

secret oaths in order to become a member. All such oaths are against God's clear command, and most are so restrictive that they are impossible for everyone to keep perfectly. Consequently, as a Christian, I believe that we need to stay away from them if we don't want to put ourselves in danger of coming under a curse.

Curses Pronounced by Others

A third way to come under a curse is to for another to pronounce the curse on another person. The best example comes from Scripture where Balak hired the prophet Balaam to pronounce upon Israel.

> Now Balak the son of Zippor saw all that Israel had done to the Amorites. And Moab was exceedingly afraid of the people because they were many, and Moab was sick with dread because of the children of Israel. So Moab said to the elders of Midian, "Now this company will lick up everything around us, as an ox licks up the grass of the field." And Balak the son of Zippor was king of the Moabites at that time. Then he sent messengers to Balaam the son of Beor at Pethor, which is near the River in the land of the sons of his people, to call him, saying: "Look, a people has come from Egypt. See, they cover the face of the earth, and are settling next to me! Therefore please come at once, curse this people for me, for they are too mighty for me. Perhaps I shall be able to defeat them and drive them out of the land, for I know that he whom you bless is blessed, and he whom you curse is cursed." (Numbers 22:2–6)

Of course, you should remember the rest of the story of how God refused to allow Balaam to curse Israel, but rather changed the words in his mouth to a blessing rather than a curse. Still, many people still pronounce a curse upon another for various reasons, usually as a method of revenge. If the person is not aware and does not resist, or openly rebuke the curse, it can happen. The problem, of course, is the power of suggestion is strong in humans, just watch someone yawn and try to resist the urge to yawn yourself! The point is that a curse can find a home in any unsuspecting or ignorant person.

During my 11 years of ministry in the remote mountains of the Philippines, I encountered the practice of cursing on a number of occasions. While it is prevalent in a number of the local tribal areas, in the late 1950's a group of American missionaries who represented the "oneness" movement evangelized these areas of the Philippines and spread their brand of Christianity. The "oneness" movement is an old doctrine that had to be dealt with by an early church council. The Council of Nicaea was the first ecumenical debate held to establish the question of who and of what did God consist. Their conclusion was that the Godhead consists of three persons, completely moving as one, but separate. Its goal was to establish the relationship of God the Father, God the Son, and God the Holy Spirit. The idea of the "oneness" of God has had several theologies develop over the centuries, but the one in the Philippines generally teaches that there is only one God who operates in three different "modes". In other words, God will manifest Himself one day as the Father, but the exact same person will manifest Himself the next day as the Son, or maybe God the Holy Spirit, but they are not three persons, but only one. Because of that, to be saved one must be baptized in the name of Jesus only, and not the formula that Jesus gave the disciples; "in the name of the Father and of the Son and of the Holy Spirit" (Matthew 28:19b). Therefore, if you do, or ever have belonged to the oneness church, you cannot leave, or you are cursed. If fact, because Jesus instructed His disciples that when they went into a town to evangelize it,

> (a)nd whoever will not receive you nor hear your words, when you depart from that house or city, shake off the dust from your feet. Assuredly, I say to you, it will be more tolerable for the land of Sodom and Gomorrah in the day of judgment than for that city! (Matthew 10:14–15)

Which of course, it is obvious that they were pronouncing a curse against them. Well, that is exactly what these "oneness" people do. If you don't believe their teaching or leave their congregation, they will literally send a representative to your house and try to convert you. If you won't accept it, they will pronounce a curse against you, shake their feet to knock off any dust from their shoes and walk out of the house. People who are not strong believers and are ignorant of the devices of the devil, can fear to the point of it affecting their conscience and thereby open themselves up to receive the curse. Paul seems to say that one who is ignorant of the devices of the devil can fall prey to him. "(L)est Satan should take advantage of us; for we are not ignorant of his devices." (2 Corinthians 2:11).

Willful Submission of Oneself To Satan or Demon

Another main reason for demonic control in an individual is the willful submission of oneself to Satan or one of his demons in exchange for some "favor" or benefit. A very popular theme for movies over the past 75 years has been of someone who sold their soul to the devil in exchange for some benefit. For example, in the movie "Love of the Damned" (2000), a man sells his soul in order to get revenge on the people who killed his girlfriend. In return the devil turned him into a demon. In another movie made in 2007, a young stunt rider sells his soul to a demon named Mephisto in exchange for having his father's cancer cured. And of course, there is the story of Robert Johnson who was born in 1911 in Hazlehurst, Mississippi, who sold his soul to the devil in exchange for musical success and fortune. And countless more examples. Temptation is a fact of life and we always have a choice when tempted. Jesus was familiar with temptation because Scripture reveals that He "was in all points tempted as we are, yet without sin" (Hebrews 4:15b).

The fact of the matter is that people sell their souls to the devil, sometimes literally and knowingly, and sometimes ignorantly not realizing that it is a literal possibility to do so. Whatever the case, Satan is still roaming around the world, and has countless numbers of his helper demons roaming around the world too, just looking for someone to deceive. And he is surprisingly successfully in achieving his goal. Sports and entertainment have always been popular activities and breeds strong competition and often hostility toward any competitor. Consequently, sports and entertainment are ripe fields for demonic activity. A lot of people will sell their souls in exchange for glory, money, power, or pleasure. A discerning person will recognize these as the very things Satan tempted Jesus with, only Jesus resisted all of them. "And the devil said to Him, "If You are the Son of God, command this stone to become bread." But Jesus answered him, saying, "It is written, 'Man shall not live by bread alone, but by every word of God'" (Luke 4:3–4). Unfortunately, Satan has not changed his tactics and it has proved successful for him.

One of the gifts of the Spirit is the "discerning of spirits" (1 Corinthians 12:10b), and it is of utmost importance for believers to exercise that gift, because Satan is working overtime to deceive you and oftentimes, he does that through temptation. Satan cannot read your mind, but he is good at reading your reactions. When he plants a thought in your mind, or presents you with some attractive offer, he watches closely to see your reaction. And if he notices a positive reaction, or some sign of interest, then he knows that he has tempted you and you need to be able to discern his activity in your life. For this reason, we are told to "resist the devil and he will flee from you" (James 4:7b).

During Unconsciousness or Altered Consciousness

The last reason I want to discuss as a cause for falling under demonic control is those times when a person goes through some traumatic experience, or even in some cases during a severe accident. There are a lot of instances when, for example, a person is sent to war and undergoes one or more very traumatic experiences, like coming under direct fire, or captured and taken captive, and maybe undergoing torture. In such cases a person can come under such pressure that is literally mind-altering. There is a saying that I have heard over my lifetime for such experiences, and that is "to be scared out of your mind". And, in fact, it is possible for that to happen. Often in the past 50 years it is simply referred to as "post-traumatic stress syndrome". Now, please don't misunderstand me on this point. I am not saying that there is not a legitimate condition that is rightly diagnosed as post-traumatic stress syndrome, but what I am suggesting is that because Satan is no gentleman, he will force himself upon people under circumstances when they are the most vulnerable, and when a person is in an unbearable condition when their defenses are weakened, Satan can and will enter that individual and affect their life until such point as they can be delivered. Please don't assume that anyone who has been diagnosed with post-traumatic stress syndrome is oppressed by the devil and needs deliverance, but there are certainly some. And, again, operating the spiritual gift of the discerning of spirits will prove beneficial, both for you, the one God wants to use to deliver that person, as well as the person oppressed by demonic activity.

Another condition that the devil has been known to enter and oppress, or in some cases, possess an individual is when the person is involved in a severe accident. This is very much like experiencing post-traumatic stress syndrome in that the person's mind is affected, and Satan takes advantage of the weakened condition entering the person or oppressing them. It is so vital for Christians to operate the gifts of the Holy Spirit that were given to the church for its benefit. The gift of discerning of spirits, is essential, because, again, we have an arch enemy who is out to deceive us and cause us to fall under his influence.

Another activity that can allow demonic activity in our life is a more controversial one, and another trick the devil uses in the name of medical treatment is deep breathing. While a few deep breaths can be beneficial when a person is over stressed to calm them down, the practice when used to alter the mind's operation can be dangerous spiritually. I am referring here to the practice of breathing deeply over an extended time which will actually affect the brain similar to the way some drugs affect it and under such circumstances can open the door to demonic activity. Again, and I cannot over stress this truth, Satan is real, and his tactics are many and varied. The bottom line is that he is intent on finding and destroying Christians, and as such, we need to be vigilant to both know his ways and to resist and combat his efforts.

Now that we have spent considerable time discussing reasons for demonic control in an individual or group of people, the obvious next issue is the steps to deliverance. We must first discern the activity of the devil; know the causes; then actually deliver the person from demonic oppression or possession.

THE STEPS TO DELIVERANCE

Indication of The Need of Deliverance

Before we can successfully set a person free from demonic oppression, we must know the cause of the oppression. In other words, how did the devil get in. Now, the reason for this is because, while Satan knows very well how he got in, the individual probably does not. Except in the case where the person knowingly and deliberately made a deal with the devil for some perceived benefit, the individual probably has no idea where the oppression came from. It will be important to identify the point of entry so the person's mental facilities will be able to assist in the deliverance. Remember, Satan is not a gentleman, and will force himself on people in vulnerable situations, where God is the perfect gentleman, and will not force himself on someone. Therefore, we want the person to be knowledgeable and be a participant in deliverance. If a person is actually possessed by the devil, then they will probably have no ability to help and the demon will have to be exorcised. However, if the person is not possessed, but oppressed, which will be the majority of the cases, then the individual will have to be a participant in their deliverance, because once set free, it will be their responsibility to stay free.

The first point of entry is through some addiction. When a person is addicted to anything, they will usually do almost anything to sustain and feed their addiction. The most common addictions are nicotine, alcohol, drugs, caffeine, food and a whole host of others. Pretty much anything in life can be addictive when you give yourself to it. In fact, there was a documentary film made in 2004 called "Super Size Me", where a man ate nothing but McDonald's food for a 30-day period. He actually became addicted to the high carbohydrate food and suffered severe withdrawal symptoms at the end of his experiment. Of course, the most common addictions are to drugs, both legal and illegal ones. Too many people assume that if a drug is legal or prescribed by a doctor then it is okay to use it. Nothing could be further from the truth. In fact some of the most addictive drugs are legal when prescribed by a doctor, but when abused can become addictive, and when you become addicted to anything, you leave yourself open to demonic activity. Under an addicted mind, you become like a hostage in that you will do almost anything to have your drug. Consequently, it is important for both the victim of addiction and the person ministering deliverance to them to recognize if some addiction is the cause of the oppression.

A second area that the minister of deliverance needs to know is if the person is suffering some physical infirmity such as an uncommon disease that has no cure, or maybe some sickness that seems to be in the family line or even a sickness that cannot be healed by ordinary prayer and laying on of hands. Remember that Christians are healed by the strips Jesus bore on His way to Calvary's cross. Listen carefully to Peter's instruction to believers,

> who, when He was reviled, did not revile in return; when He suffered, He did not threaten, but committed Himself to Him who judges righteously; who Himself bore our sins in His own body on the tree, that we, having died to sins, might live for righteousness — by whose stripes you were healed. (1 Peter 2:23–25)

So, it becomes obvious that Jesus did not expect sickness to be a "normal" part of the believer's life. Now, please don't misunderstand me on this point, because I am not trying to say that a Christian should not go to a doctor or use medication for an ailment. What I am saying is what is plainly taught in Scripture and I believe that we do not want to listen to the deceptive teaching of the devil that God either can't heal today, or the more popular teaching by some that somewhere along the line, God changed His mind and simply doesn't heal anymore. If it is true, and I firmly believe it, God is the same yesterday, today and forever. If He healed yesterday, then He still heals today. Isaiah prophesied that by the strips of the promised Messiah, God's people would be healed (Isaiah, 53:5) and Peter affirmed it as pertaining to the New Testament church, then why shouldn't we as born-again Christians believe it? So, when a person is suffering from some uncurable disease, I believe that we need to look at a spiritual cause brought on by the devil and in need of a spiritual cure – deliverance from demonic attack. Don't forget the story of Job, where it is abundantly clear that Job's physical infirmity is brought on him by Satan, and only God could deliver him from it (see Job 2:7ff). The same is true today, many diseases are brought upon God's people that are brought on by the devil and his demonic forces and we as ministers of God, must be prepared to deliver God's people from these infirmities. But as long as we refuse to acknowledge Satan's activity and God's intention that we as Christian ministers are equipped to deliver such individuals, we will continue to allow Satan to work undetected undercover of his deceptive ways.

We need to examine a third area where Satan likes to hide and deceive people through religious error in such false religious practices such as found in eastern religions, Yoga, Hari Krisna, and what is called the New Age movement. As well, there are many cults in the world today that put their adherents in a vulnerable place to be deceived by the devil. Some of these deceptive cults include Mormonism, Jehovah's Witness, Iglesia ni Cristo, Moonism, Buddhism and many others. The very term "cult" carries many meanings and would mean simply a new "social movement" by some. To most Christians the term means a false religion that denies biblical truth. I am using the term here in the Christian sense, referring to religious organizations whose teachings do not follow the full teachings of the Bible. Most of them claim to adhere to the Bible but pick and choose what parts to use and which to deny or discard. For example, a very large movement in the Philippines that has attracted millions of people around the world believe the teachings of Apollo Quiboloy who claims to be the "Appointed Son of God". He pastors the movement called the Kingdom of Jesus Christ, The Name Above Every Name.

Such religious movements deceive many into believing false doctrines and steer countless numbers of people from even examining the truths of the Scriptures and in the process leave them open to believing lies which, of course, Satan loves and uses that deception to invade their life. Jesus was very clear in His teaching about such religious leaders. The Pharisees, the religious leaders of Jesus day, have this testimony from Jesus Himself.

But woe to you, scribes and Pharisees, hypocrites! For you shut up the kingdom of heaven against men; for you neither go in yourselves, nor do you allow those who are entering to go in. Woe to you, scribes and Pharisees, hypocrites! For you devour widows' houses, and for a pretense make long prayers. Therefore you will receive greater condemnation.

> Woe to you, scribes and Pharisees, hypocrites! For you travel land and sea to win one proselyte, and when he is won, you make him twice as much a son of hell as yourselves. (Matthew 23:13–15)

Notice Jesus's charge against them. They should have known better, but they deliberately taught the people their own version of the Scriptures and taught such a strict doctrine that they themselves could not even obey it, yet they would forbid the people from even considering any other way. These Pharisees were great evangelists and would literally travel the world over to make disciples. However, because every seed reproduces after its own kind, and because they were hypocrites, they produced even worse hypocrites than themselves. This is what the leaders of the cults do, they make such laws for their adherents that the people can't ever measure up nor do the leaders follow all of their own regulations that they place on everyone else.

The fact of the matter is, these cults that teach false doctrines, are tools of Satan that he uses to get influence into the lives of millions of people around the world, and thereby get a foothold to deceive millions of people. These people need faithful ministers of the gospel to speak truth into their lives and when a person sees the error of their way, many will need individual deliverance. There is a desperate need in the world for people called to the deliverance ministry to minister to people caught in the trap of deception by the devil and his hordes of evil demons. Paul warned Timothy of such people who Satan uses to deceive the world.

Now the Spirit expressly says that in latter times some will depart from the faith, giving heed to deceiving spirits and doctrines of demons, speaking lies in hypocrisy, having their own conscience seared with a hot iron, forbidding to marry, and commanding to abstain from foods which God created to be received with thanksgiving by those who believe and know the truth. (1 Timothy 4:1–3)

And then in his second letter, he warned Timothy in even more specific terms of the danger.

But know this, that in the last days perilous times will come: For men will be lovers of themselves, lovers of money, boasters, proud, blasphemers, disobedient to parents, unthankful, unholy, unloving, unforgiving, slanderers, without self-control, brutal, despisers of good, traitors, headstrong, haughty, lovers of pleasure rather than lovers of God, having a form of godliness but denying its power. And from such people turn away! For of this sort are those who creep into households and make captives of gullible women loaded down with sins, led away by various lusts, always learning and never able to come to the knowledge of the truth. Now as Jannes and Jambres resisted Moses, so do these also resist the truth: men of corrupt minds, disapproved concerning the faith; but they will progress no further, for their folly will be manifest to all, as theirs also was. (2 Timothy 3:1–9)

The point is clear, in the last days, and who can deny that in the 21st century we are indeed living in the last days; many false teachings come along designed specifically by Satan to deceive the masses and draw people away from God's true church who teaches His true Word. A true minister of Jesus Christ will be aware of this movement by Satan and be available to set people free from such deceptive bondage. But now it is time to move on to a discussion on the basis of deliverance.

The Basis of Deliverance

I am hoping that the reader has already concluded that the basis of any level of deliverance from Satan's influence has to be Christ and His finished work on the cross. As in every area of theological debate, I intend to let Scripture speak for itself. I want to allow John, Peter, Paul and the writer of the book of Hebrews to speak to this issue. First, listen to what John had to say concerning the works of the devil.

> "Little children, let no one deceive you. He who practices righteousness is righteous, just as He is righteous. He who sins is of the devil, for the devil has sinned from the beginning. For this purpose the Son of God was manifested, that He might destroy the works of the devil" (1 John 3:7–8).

And then it is important to understand what the writer of Hebrews had to say about the works of the devil.

> In as much then as the children have partaken of flesh and blood, He Himself likewise shared in the same, that through death He might destroy him who had the power of death, that is, the devil, and release those who through fear of death were all their lifetime subject to bondage. (Hebrews 2:14–15).

Their point is clear, Satan is come to lie and deceive anyone who would desire to turn to God and His Son Jesus Christ for deliverance and salvation. It was for this precise reason that Jesus left His first estate at the right hand of God, as God to came into the world to defeat the one being who's only desire was to kill and destroy anything of God. But Peter also weighed in on the debate when he said that Jesus provided deliverance for God's people.

And if you call on the Father, who without partiality judges according to each one's work, conduct yourselves throughout the time of your stay here in fear; knowing that you were not redeemed with corruptible things, like silver or gold, from your aimless conduct received by tradition from your fathers, but with the precious blood of Christ, as of a lamb without blemish and without spot. He indeed was foreordained before the foundation of the world, but was manifest in these last times for you who through Him believe in God, who raised Him from the dead and gave Him glory, so that your faith and hope are in God. (1 Peter 1:17–21)

And then we have the word given to us by Paul about what Christ accomplished for us on Calvary's cross.

For as many as are of the works of the law are under the curse; for it is written, "Cursed is everyone who does not continue in all things which are written in the book of the law, to do them." But that no one is justified by the law in the sight of God is evident, for "the just shall live by faith." Yet the law is not of faith, but "the man who does them shall live by them."

> Christ has redeemed us from the curse of the law, having become a curse for us (for it is written, "Cursed is everyone who hangs on a tree"), that the blessing of Abraham might come upon the Gentiles in Christ Jesus, that we might receive the promise of the Spirit through faith. (Galatians 3:10–14)

So, we have been set free from the curse, and the curse is administered by Satan. It is by and through Christ that we have been set free and it is up to us to simply believe. Remember what Abraham did to gain God's favor and be counted righteous, that is eligible to be accepted into God's presence. He simply believed God "and He accounted it to him for righteousness" (Genesis 15:6b). And that is all He asks of us as well to be accepted by Him as worthy to be accepted into His presence.

While it might be possible to write an entire book on the subject of deliverance from demonic control and influence, I want to conclude this chapter with a quick overview of the need and the general approach to the deliverance ministry. It must be entered into with knowledge, faith, and compassion.

An indication of the need of deliverance will include things like emotional problems, such as an emotional disturbance in the feelings, like hatred, resentment, anger, fear, rejection, self-pity, jealousy, worry, inferiority, and others. It would also include mental problems; disturbances in the thought life such as mental torment, procrastination, indecision, compromise, confusion, doubt, rationalization and loss of memory. Another indication of the need for deliverance might include speech problems like an outburst or uncontrolled use of the tongue, lying, cursing, blasphemy, criticism, mockery, gossip, boasting. And finally, a number of sex problems would indicate a need for deliverance from demonic attack. These might include such things as recurring unclean thoughts and acts regarding sex like engaging in a fantasy sex experience, masturbation, lust, perversions, homosexuality, fornication, adultery, incest, provocativeness, prostitution, frigidity, and others.

The bottom line is Satan is a real enemy and will try his best to influence you in some way to engage in evil. We, as Christians have been given the knowledge and the tools to resist him and escape his attacks. We have been given the full armor of God to overcome any attack he might wage against us. However, once a person gives in to one of his lies and comes under his influence, many times a person needs help to find deliverance. And God has called and equipped some just for that purpose. Deliverance is one of the ministries Jesus was commissioned to accomplish, and He has commissioned some of you to be engaged in the same ministry.

> The Spirit of the Lord is upon Me,
> Because He has anointed Me
> To preach the gospel to the poor;
> He has sent Me to heal the brokenhearted,
> To proclaim liberty to the captives
> And recovery of sight to the blind,
> To set at liberty those who are oppressed;
> To proclaim the acceptable year of the Lord." (Luke 4:18–19)

Notice Jesus was sent to set at liberty those who are oppressed, and there is only one oppressor, and that is Satan. Are you called to set at liberty those who are oppressed by our arch enemy?

The ministry of deliverance is one of the ministries of the Church. Like all other ministries, it is the LORD who calls, equips and anoints the one ministering. It is not a higher ministry, but it is an important ministry in the church. It is not to be entered into lightly. It requires commitment and dedication.

5

THE COVENANTS OF GOD AND HIS FAITHFULNESS TO THEM

INTRODUCTION

G **od is known** as the covenant making God, and rightly so because He established a covenant with certain people throughout history, and the current time is no different. We see the first covenant with Adam at creation and then, of course, the covenant He made with Noah. From there He made a covenant with Abraham and his "seed", and renewed it with his son Isaac, and finally with Isaac's son Jacob. He renewed and expanded the covenant with Abraham to David, the man after God's own heart, and his "seed", which Scripture makes clear was Jesus the Christ of God, who actually fulfilled the covenant made with Abraham. I want to explore each of these covenants that God made and show that we as born-again Christians are recipients of these covenants when we "abide" in Christ.

Briefly stated, all the covenants of God are related and tied together by God's Word which is based on truth and faithfulness. God is faithful and will never lie to His people or renege on any of His promises; we can count on Him to keep all of the provisions of His covenant for all time. First, is His covenant with Adam, which had both temporal and eternal qualities to it. It was temporal in that much of the promise was conditional in that it was based on Adam keeping God's requirements and not eating of the fruit of the Tree of Good and Evil. It was eternal in that God is a faithful and just God whose actions toward His creation are based on love as well as justice. So, when they sinned, God's justice demanded that they die spiritually, but His love demanded that He provide a way to redeem them.

It is important that Christians study and understand the covenants so we can understand our God better, but to also be able to better understand the end of humanity in light of the beginning. God is the same yesterday, today and forever (Hebrews 13:8), therefore we can more clearly understand how He relates to His people and how we can expect Him to react to us in various conditions in the future. One other important purpose in studying and understanding the covenants of God is because they are a progressive expression of the image of God, which is the major characteristic of the Spirit of God which we are given when we believe in His work and provision for us. In more familiar language, we begin receiving His progressive revelation when we are born-again of the Spirit of God. And yet another important point to understand about God's covenants is that they have all been mediated through humanity. That is, He has always used a specific person who He deemed faithful through whom to mediate the covenant. For example, when He made the covenant with Adam, the covenant did not just apply to him and his wife, but to all of humanity. When Adam ate the fruit and died, all of those who would come from him died also. From the point of sinning when Adam's spirit died, everyone born to him and their descendants were born without a spirit and were only body and soul. And ever since that time mankind has had an "empty spot" in themselves and have sought various ways to fill that void. Nevertheless, God did not abandon His creation, but immediately begin to encourage His people to seek after Him. He accomplished that by way of justice administered as judgment on sin, and covenant promises, whereby He promised to restore a people unto Himself and to save them in the end.

His goal in initiating covenants through humanity and with humanity was the progressive glorification of humanity by God's grace, the result being the maturing of all creation through the final recipient of His covenant promise, His very own, only begotten Son, Jesus Christ.

Listen carefully to Paul's explanation of God's plan and purpose through the covenants He made with His creation.

> For I consider that the sufferings of this present time are not worthy to be compared with the glory which shall be revealed in us. For the earnest expectation of the creation eagerly waits for the revealing of the sons of God. For the creation was subjected to futility, not willingly, but because of Him who subjected it in hope; because the creation itself also will be delivered from the bondage of corruption into the glorious liberty of the children of God. For we know that the whole creation groans and labors with birth pangs together until now. Not only that, but we also who have the firstfruits of the Spirit, even we ourselves groan within ourselves, eagerly waiting for the adoption, the redemption of our body. For we were saved in this hope, but hope that is seen is not hope; for why does one still hope for what he sees? But if we hope for what we do not see, we eagerly wait for it with perseverance (Romans 8:18–25).

So, Paul is clear, the entire creation is under the bondage of the curse that Adam brought upon it when he sinned by partaking of the fruit of the forbidden tree. He then experienced the death of his spirit, and the corruption of the entire world. It should be clear from the discussion so far that the entire creation, including mankind, animals, and even the environment will be set free and restored to its perfect condition that God initially created. Remember that when God finished creating the world, the Scripture records, "Then God saw everything that He had made, and indeed it was very good" (Genesis 1:31). It was only sin that caused corruption, and the final fulfillment of God's covenant is the full restoration of His entire creation. Now one more truth that we have to fully understand as we begin our study of God's covenants with His creation and that is our final state. We need to understand God's plan so we need to refute a popular doctrine that is circulating in certain parts of the church. When we are fully restored with the Spirit of God, we do not become gods ourselves. We are restored in the image and likeness of God by becoming new creatures, becoming Christlike, but not Christs. We will never become God or gods', but we will be engaged in an ongoing growing and maturing process whereby we exhibit more and more Christlike characteristics.

Let's take a closer look at each of the covenants – what they entailed and the result or fulfillment of that covenant. Remember, as I mentioned earlier, some of the covenants were temporary and conditional, while one covenant in particular wat unconditional and eternal. The one was for the people to whom God made it as well as all future people who were meant to be recipients of it.

GOD'S COVENANT WITH ADAM

I already covered some of the provisions of the covenant God made with Adam in the introduction to this chapter. Nevertheless, I need to elaborate on a few points because it is important to understand God's plan, His purpose, and what we can do today to fulfill our part in God's plan. I taught apologetics at a Bible College for many years and one of the first questions skeptics would always ask as well as one many committed Bible College students would often ask is "Why would a good God as revealed to us in Scripture allow such bad things to happen to good people?" That is a very good question and it is asked by some out of defense for their not believing, and others ask sincerely out of a sincere desire to know because they are suffering terribly or know someone who is suffering even when following God with all their heart. Without understanding the events that led to this condition, we will never be able to answer such questions.

To help us understand, we have to look carefully at what God did and what He said to Adam when he was created, formed, and given the breath of life, given Eve as a companion and given the Garden of Eden as a home.

> And the Lord God commanded the man, saying, "Of every
> tree of the garden you may freely eat; but of the tree of the

> knowledge of good and evil you shall not eat, for in the day
> that you eat of it you shall surely die" (Genesis 2:16–17).

Notice carefully God's condition for the promise/covenant that He made with them. First, He promised them the Garden as a home, which God had just prepared as a "very good" home free of any corruption, with a Tree of Life placed in the center of the Garden that would continually give life to these humans who were living and reproducing on the earth as long as they obeyed God and resisted partaking of the one forbidden tree. But there was this one condition and the condition involved either life or death. Now the one thing that is not as clear in the covenant was the fact that it was not just them that would die, but all of this "very good" creation of God would be affected and suffer from the consequences of their disobedience. When the human spirit of Adam and Eve died, or as it is referred to in theology, when Adam and Eve "fell", so did all of creation. The fall affected all of creation, mankind as well as their environment. Adam and Eve suffered the slow gradual death of their body and all of creation began the process of decay which involved the introduction of thorns and weeds that would compete with the good seed for nutrients to grow and produce fruit in the earth. The fall also began the process of the deterioration of the environment with violent storms, floods, earthquakes and extreme weather in various places. This, of course, is what Paul was talking about when he said, "For we know that the whole creation groans and labors with birth pangs together until now" (Romans 8:22). I hope each reader can understand why it is important to understand the Adamic covenant in order to help explain why creation, created good by a good God is in the corrupted state that it is today.

The next objection might be "Why then would an all-powerful God not simply step into history and intervene to make Adam's wrong right?" After all, He did immediately set a plan for redemption and forgiveness into motion, so why didn't He do it sooner? Actually, Paul teaches that "just as He chose us in Him before the foundation of the world, that we should be holy and without blame before Him in love, having predestined us to adoption as sons by Jesus Christ to Himself, according to the good pleasure of His will," (Ephesians 1:4–5). The reality is that God knew beforehand that Adam would sin and fall, so He set the plan in motion before He even created mankind. And because God is a just God, He could not just take back the dominion that He had given to Adam. The gifts and calling of God are irrevocable (Romans 11:29), so He was not about to steal it back, rather He devised a plan to get it back legally. Obviously, that was the only course of action for a just God. In chapter 1 we determined that the confrontation in the Garden with the serpent/the devil was not about the fruit in any way. The issue was dominion, or control over God's creation. Therefore, when Adam partook of the fruit of the forbidden tree, what was at stake was his dominion over creation, and once he gave it away, it then legally became Satan's and the only way for God to regain control was to pay the price for sin which according to Scripture is very clear, "For the wages of sin is death" (Romans 6:23). Nevertheless, Peter makes it abundantly clear that God's plan of redemption had an answer for those wages; "For He made Him who knew no sin to be sin for us, that we might become the righteousness of God in Him" (2 Corinthians 5:21).

We need to follow God's plan of redemption another step to fully understand His plan and purpose. Peter teaches us that Jesus did indeed regain dominion over God's creation when he says in 1 Peter 4:11 "that in all things God may be glorified through Jesus Christ, to whom belong the glory and the dominion forever and ever. Amen." So, when Jesus died on the cross many years later, that was the wages for Adam's sin and Jesus legally reclaimed the dominion that was originally given to Adam and Eve at creation. It should now become abundantly clear that this is why Jesus taught that we must abide in Him.

> Abide in Me, and I in you. As the branch cannot bear fruit of itself, unless it abides in the vine, neither can you, unless you abide in Me.
>
> I am the vine, you are the branches. He who abides in Me, and I in him, bears much fruit; for without Me you can do nothing. If anyone does not abide in Me, he is cast out as a branch and is withered; and they gather them and throw them into the fire, and they are burned. If you abide in

Me, and My words abide in you, you will ask what you desire, and it shall be done for you. By this My Father is glorified, that you bear much fruit; so you will be My disciples (John 15:4–8).

His point of course is that He regained dominion and the way we get the dominion that was granted to Adam and Eve is to abide in Him. Only when we abide in Him and He abides in us, by way of His Holy Spirit do we have dominion over God's creation. This becomes obvious when we witness Jesus calm the sea, stop a storm, raise the dead, and multiply the fish and loaves, and give eternal life to those who come to Him.

GOD'S COVENANT WITH NOAH

As we proceed looking at each of the covenants God made with mankind, we need to understand that God's plan is a progressive revelation of Himself. A truly Christian eschatology[19] has to be dynamic, that is, it is living, growing and changing. A static eschatology is not a Christian philosophy in any way. God is living and powerful and while He remains the same yesterday, today and forever (Hebrews 13:8), He is never idle but every moment active in the affairs of His creation. Understand that God's plan is not to simply restore creation including mankind back to what they were at creation, but to take His creation beyond Eden. Understand that the creation that was experienced at creation was just the beginning of God's plan for them. God had a work for Adam and Eve and their posterity, but that plan was interrupted by their sin and fall, therefore God has spent the time between their fall and the sending of His Son Jesus to set the stage for the redemption of His fallen creation. We do not yet see its full restoration, but we do see Jesus sitting at God the

---

[19] A branch of theology concerned with the final events in the history of the world or of humankind I introduce this term here because all of God's covenants are concerned about His dealing with creation throughout history all the way to death and eternal destiny.

Father's right hand until all His enemies are put under Him. The writer of Hebrews tries to explain this reality when he says,

You have put all things in subjection under his feet."

For in that He put all in subjection under him, He left nothing that is not put under him. But now we do not yet see all things put under him. But we see Jesus, who was made a little lower than the angels, for the suffering of death crowned with glory and honor, that He, by the grace of God, might taste death for everyone (Hebrews 2:8–9).

It becomes evident then, that God's plan in each of His covenants is that He intends to progressively reveal Himself and to progressively restore mankind to his/her original position so He can take them throughout eternity, ever moving forward. This is precisely why John said

Behold what manner of love the Father has bestowed on us, that we should be called children of God! Therefore, the world does not know us, because it did not know Him. Beloved, now we are children of God; and it has not yet been revealed what we shall be, but we know that when He is revealed, we shall be like Him, for we shall see Him as He is (1 John 3:1–2)

Where God wants to take us is so far above what we can think or imagine that John simply said "it has not yet been revealed what we shall be" (v. 2a). Nevertheless, one thing we can know is that when that day comes, "we shall be like Him" (v. 2b)!

Consequently, the covenant with Noah was rather simple. Be obedient to Me, build an ark so I can preserve a line through which I can raise up a family through whom I can bring forth the One who will fulfill all my justice and provide the means whereby I can restore a people to Myself. Trying not to speculate on what that plan might involve, I can honestly say that a God who would go to all the trouble He had to endure to provide our redemption and salvation, it has to be good, or as God Himself said about His creation, "very good!"

It is interesting that the covenant with Noah is the first time in the Bible where the word "covenant" is used. I want to walk you through this simple covenant which is found in Genesis chapter 6.

> Then the Lord saw that the wickedness of man was great in the earth, and that every intent of the thoughts of his heart was only evil continually. And the Lord was sorry that He had made man on the earth, and He was grieved in His heart. So the Lord said, "I will destroy man whom I have created from the face of the earth, both man and beast, creeping thing and birds of the air, for I am sorry that I have made them." But Noah found grace in the eyes of the Lord (vv 5–8).

And then it is recorded that "(t)his is the genealogy of Noah. Noah was a just man, perfect in his generations. Noah walked with God" (v 9). And because Noah was a just man and God could trust him to obey God made a covenant with him.

> But I will establish My covenant with you; and you shall go into the ark — you, your sons, your wife, and your sons' wives with you. And of every living thing of all flesh you shall bring two of every sort into the ark, to keep them alive with you; they shall be male and female. Of the birds after their kind, of animals after their kind, and of every creeping thing of the earth after its kind, two of every kind will come to you to keep them alive. And you shall take for yourself of all food that is eaten, and you shall gather it to yourself; and it shall be food for you and for them." (vv 18–21).

And of course, the result was successful and Noah fulfilled the terms of the covenant and God preserved a seed in the earth. "Thus Noah did; according to all that God commanded him, so he did" (v 22).

GOD'S COVENANT WITH ABRAHAM

Now we move on to the covenant God made with Abraham. This is probably the most important and long-lasting covenant God ever made. While each covenant is important and relevant to understanding a holy God, this is the covenant that the New Testament teaches is the foundation for the new covenant that we as born-again Christians enjoy the benefits of today because Jesus is the "seed" of Abraham that was the fulfillment of this covenant. Listen to Peter teach this important truth in his first Epistle.

> For Christ also suffered once for sins, the just for the unjust, that He might bring us to God, being put to death in the flesh but made alive by the Spirit, by whom also He went and preached to the spirits in prison, who formerly were disobedient, when once the Divine longsuffering waited in the days of Noah, while the ark was being prepared, in which a few, that is, eight souls, were saved through water. There is also an antitype which now saves us — baptism (not the removal of the filth of the flesh, but the answer of a good conscience toward God), through the resurrection of Jesus Christ, who has gone into heaven and is at the right hand of God, angels and authorities and powers having been made subject to Him. (1 Peter 3:18–22)

The covenant with Abraham began way back in Genesis 12, but again, as with God's overall plan, it was a progressive revelation as to the provisions of the covenant. The initial terms of the covenant are stated in Genesis 12.

Now the Lord had said to Abram:

> "Get out of your country,
> From your family
> And from your father's house,

> To a land that I will show you.
> I will make you a great nation;
> I will bless you
> And make your name great;
> And you shall be a blessing.
> I will bless those who bless you,
> And I will curse him who curses you;
> And in you all the families of the earth shall be blessed"
> (Genesis 12:1–3).

This covenant introduces a new means of administration of God's dealings with mankind and is meant to preserve a holy nation and keep the other nations at bay, until such time as the promise is fulfilled. God expanded the covenant somewhat in Genesis chapter 13.

> And the Lord said to Abram, after Lot had separated from him: "Lift your eyes now and look from the place where you are — northward, southward, eastward, and westward; for all the land which you see I give to you and your descendants forever. And I will make your descendants as the dust of the earth; so that if a man could number the dust of the earth, then your descendants also could be numbered. Arise, walk in the land through its length and its width, for I give it to you." (Genesis 13:14–17)

And then in chapter 15 is where God gets very specific and reviews the terms of the covenant and then seals the deal with an elaborate ceremony of signing and notarizing the contract.

> After these things the word of the Lord came to Abram in a vision, saying, "Do not be afraid, Abram. I am your shield, your exceedingly great reward."
>
> But Abram said, "Lord God, what will You give me, seeing I go childless, and the heir of my house is Eliezer of

Damascus?" Then Abram said, "Look, You have given me no offspring; indeed one born in my house is my heir!"

And behold, the word of the Lord came to him, saying, "This one shall not be your heir, but one who will come from your own body shall be your heir." Then He brought him outside and said, "Look now toward heaven, and count the stars if you are able to number them." And He said to him, "So shall your descendants be."

And he believed in the Lord, and He accounted it to him for righteousness.

Then He said to him, "I am the Lord, who brought you out of Ur of the Chaldeans, to give you this land to inherit it."

And he said, "Lord God, how shall I know that I will inherit it?" (Genesis 15:1–8)

Now it is time to pay special attention to how the contract is finalized. I explained some of this procedure in an earlier chapter, but it is worth repeating and elaborating on it here so there can be no misunderstanding. Most of us are familiar with how a contract is entered into today, but in Abraham's day things were radically different. Today, the parties, usually two people or entities, go to a lawyer or a qualified professional who will type up the terms of the contract and have the parties review it. When it is agreed upon by all parties, it is signed with a notary public witnessing the signing and the notary signs that the parties entered into the agreement voluntarily without duress, and it was in fact the real persons agreeing to the terms of the agreement. However, in Abraham's day the common procedure was for the two parties to agree on the terms of the agreement, usually with witnesses. When they reached agreement, they would kill an animal and cut it in half and place one half on one side of a narrow path and the other half on the other side of a narrow path. Then the two parties would both walk the narrow path between the two halves of the dead animal while calling down curses on themselves if either one would dare not fulfill all the terms of their agreement. The curse that they would call down on themselves simply stated that "if I should ever break any part of this agreement, then may the same thing that happened to this mutilated animal happen to me."

With that cultural understanding in mind, listen carefully to how God "signed" this agreement that Him and Abraham were entering into.

> So He said to him, "Bring Me a three-year-old heifer, a three-year-old female goat, a three-year-old ram, a turtledove, and a young pigeon." Then he brought all these to Him and cut them in two, down the middle, and placed each piece opposite the other; but he did not cut the birds in two. And when the vultures came down on the carcasses, Abram drove them away (Genesis 15:9–11).

Notice that God did not just have Abraham slaughter one animal, but he literally slaughtered three animals plus two birds that were then placed half on each side of a narrow path with one whole dead bird placed on each side as well. When it comes time to ratify the covenant by having the two parties walk the path between the dead carcasses, we have to pay special attention because that is the key to understanding how this covenant pertains to us as born-again Christians today. I am personally convinced that a misunderstanding of this covenant is the basis for a lot of division in the body of Christ today. Therefore, look for the whereabouts of each participant as the covenant is ratified.

> Now when the sun was going down, a deep sleep fell upon Abram; and behold, horror and great darkness fell upon him. Then He said to Abram: "Know certainly that your descendants will be strangers in a land that is not theirs, and will serve them, and they will afflict them four hundred years. And also the nation whom they serve I will judge; afterward they shall come out with great possessions. Now as for you, you shall go to your fathers

in peace; you shall be buried at a good old age. But in the fourth generation they shall return here, for the iniquity of the Amorites is not yet complete."

And it came to pass, when the sun went down and it was dark, that behold, there appeared a smoking oven and a burning torch that passed between those pieces. On the same day the Lord made a covenant with Abram, saying:

"To your descendants I have given this land, from the river of Egypt to the great river, the River Euphrates — the Kenites, the Kenezzites, the Kadmonites, the Hittites, the Perizzites, the Rephaim, the Amorites, the Canaanites, the Girgashites, and the Jebusites." (Genesis 15:12–21).

I trust that you noticed that Abraham was sound asleep while he had a vision of God walking down that narrow path with all the mutilated dead animals all alone. I hope you are asking the vital question, "Why?" At this point it is important to remember the covenant God made with Adam. According to the terms of that covenant, Adam had to fulfill his part in the covenant which was to perfectly obey the command of the Lord or the covenant would be null and void. Of course, we all know that Adam did not keep his part, therefore he came under the curse that was a provision of the normal part of the oath taking of entering into a covenant. When Adam broke the terms of the covenant, God was released from His part of the contract as well. Consequently, God knowing that "the wickedness of man was great in the earth, and that every intent of the thoughts of his heart was only evil continually" (Genesis 6:5), determined that He was not going to take any chances on mankind again, He bypassed Abraham and ratified the covenant without him. "For when God made a promise to Abraham, because He could swear by no one greater, He swore by Himself, saying, "Surely blessing I will bless you, and multiplying I will multiply you"" (Hebrews 6:13–14).

Now we need to continue searching Scripture to discover that this covenant that God swore to by Himself, and since "God is not a man, that he should lie" (Numbers 23:19a), we can absolutely rely on Him to fulfill that covenant with His people. We also need to understand that this covenant has several aspects to it. First, it had personal aspects because God promised to bless Abraham ("I will bless you" Genesis 12:2b) and He promised to grant him a great reputation ("and make your name great (v 12:2c), and as well it had punitive protection included for Abraham, "And I will curse him who curses you" (v. 3b). We learn from Paul in the New Testament that this is the very covenant that pointed to Jesus and anyone who is born-again of the Spirit that Jesus provided upon His ascension into heaven. Pay careful attention as Paul explains –

> Christ has redeemed us from the curse of the law, having become a curse for us (for it is written, "Cursed is everyone who hangs on a tree"), that the blessing of Abraham might come upon the Gentiles in Christ Jesus, that we might receive the promise of the Spirit through faith.

> Brethren, I speak in the manner of men: Though it is only a man's covenant, yet if it is confirmed, no one annuls or adds to it. Now to Abraham and his Seed were the promises made. He does not say, "And to seeds," as of many, but as of one, "And to your Seed," who is Christ. And this I say, that the law, which was four hundred and thirty years later, cannot annul the covenant that was confirmed before by God in Christ, that it should make the promise of no effect. For if the inheritance is of the law, it is no longer of promise; but God gave it to Abraham by promise. (Galatians 3:13–18)

It is at this point that there is some controversy as well as some confusion because the term "seed" when used as offspring, can mean one or many. It is obvious that in one sense, and as Abraham must have understood it, God was referring to all of his offspring, because when he confronted God with the argument "Lord God, what will You give me, seeing I go childless, and the heir of my house is Eliezer of Damascus?" Then Abram said, "Look, You have given me no offspring; indeed one born in my house is my heir!" (Genesis 15:2–3), he was obviously concerned about all of his posterity. However, remember from our discussion elsewhere that God had to keep His ultimate purpose and plan a deep secret lest Satan find out about it and was successful at thwarting it. Consequently, we don't discover until the New Testament that God was referring not only to Abraham's physical offspring, but also concerning his spiritual offspring. Again, Paul is helpful in explaining the difference between the physical and spiritual offspring of Abraham in Romans 9.

> But it is not that the word of God has taken no effect. For they are not all Israel who are of Israel, nor are they all children because they are the seed of Abraham; but, "In Isaac your seed shall be called." That is, those who are the children of the flesh, these are not the children of God; but the children of the promise are counted as the seed. For this is the word of promise: "At this time I will come and Sarah shall have a son."
>
> And not only this, but when Rebecca also had conceived by one man, even by our father Isaac (for the children not yet being born, nor having done any good or evil, that the purpose of God according to election might stand, not of works but of Him who calls), it was said to her, "The older shall serve the younger." As it is written, "Jacob I have loved, but Esau I have hated." (Romans 9:6–13)

And when we think about it and we consider the history of God's dealings with mankind it becomes much clearer. Out of all the people on the earth, God began with Adam and Eve, bypassed Cain and Abel, began again with Seth, then all the way to Noah, then bypassing Noah's two other sons, picked up with Shem and then on to Abraham, Isaac, and Jacob (Israel), then bypassing Jacob's other 11 sons, He chooses Judah, then He proceeds to choose David and then all the way forward to Christ, the elect "seed". In other words, we can only partake of the promise of God through Christ.

When we finally realize what God did and that this covenant that He made with Abraham is ours as well, we will have such security in Christ that we can truly rejoice in the salvation of the Lord. Remember that because God could swear to uphold the requirements of this covenant that He made to us through Christ, He swore by Himself that if He should ever renege on any of the provisions of this covenant, the curses that are a part of the covenant will come upon Him, and we KNOW that that will never happen. Therefore, we are secure in Christ!

GOD'S COVENANT WITH MOSES

Now as we move forward to the covenant God made with Moses, which included the entire nation of Israel, the physical "seed" of Abraham, we discover immediately that it was in fact a temporary conditional covenant, similar in many ways to the very first covenant God made with Adam. It was conditional in that it contained both specific consequences for obedience as well as disobedience. It was a temporary covenant because God had already made the permanent covenant with Abraham and, as Paul so aptly points out, no one can override that permanent covenant.

> And this I say, that the law, which was four hundred and thirty years later, cannot annul the covenant that was confirmed before by God in Christ, that it should make the promise of no effect. For if the inheritance is of the law, it is no longer of promise; but God gave it to Abraham by promise (Galatians 3:17–18).

And it was conditional because there were thousands of very specific laws and statutes that were required to be obeyed in order to qualify for the blessings promised for absolute obedience. Nevertheless, there were also many curses to be endured if they failed to obey the law perfectly.

Remember with the covenant God made with Abraham, God put Abraham to sleep and swore allegiance to the promise by Himself, so He alone was responsible to uphold all the provisions of the covenant. With this covenant however, both God and the people were involved in making it and it was God who established the terms of the covenant, but He required the people to ratify it, making them responsible for upholding its terms as well as Him. Because Joshua was Moses's assistant and accompanied Him up on the mountain and in the tabernacle, he knew God well enough and had witnessed the rebellious behavior of the people long enough, that he knew the people would not be able to perfectly obey the law. However, the people insisted that they could and signed the covenant with God vowing to obey all the law. For this reason, after Moses died and Joshua led Israel across the Jorden River and Israel conquered the land, when Joshua was ready to die, he made the people ratify the law.

> But Joshua said to the people, "You cannot serve the Lord, for He is a holy God. He is a jealous God; He will not forgive your transgressions nor your sins. If you forsake the Lord and serve foreign gods, then He will turn and do you harm and consume you, after He has done you good."
>
> And the people said to Joshua, "No, but we will serve the Lord!"
>
> So Joshua said to the people, "You are witnesses against yourselves that you have chosen the Lord for yourselves, to serve Him."
>
> And they said, "We are witnesses!" (Joshua 24:19–22)

Now I want to look specifically at the terms of this covenant God made with Israel along with both the blessings for obedience and the curses for disobedience. We also need to explore the purpose of this covenant and the result along with some principles we can glean from it for our life in the twenty-first century. While they are listed in several places, I want to focus on the words of Moses in Deuteronomy chapter 28. Here he summarizes the terms of the covenant and is much more precise than in other accounts. First the promises for complete obedience to the law.

> Now it shall come to pass, if you diligently obey the voice of the Lord your God, to observe carefully all His commandments which I command you today, that the Lord your God will set you high above all nations of the earth. And all these blessings shall come upon you and overtake you, because you obey the voice of the Lord your God:
>
> "Blessed shall you be in the city, and blessed shall you be in the country.
>
> "Blessed shall be the fruit of your body, the produce of your ground and the increase of your herds, the increase of your cattle and the offspring of your flocks.
>
> "Blessed shall be your basket and your kneading bowl.
>
> "Blessed shall you be when you come in, and blessed shall you be when you go out.
>
> "The Lord will cause your enemies who rise against you to be defeated before your face; they shall come out against you one way and flee before you seven ways.
>
> "The Lord will command the blessing on you in your storehouses and in all to which you set your hand, and He will bless you in the land which the Lord your God is giving you.

"The Lord will establish you as a holy people to Himself, just as He has sworn to you, if you keep the commandments of the Lord your God and walk in His ways. Then all peoples of the earth shall see that you are called by the name of the Lord, and they shall be afraid of you. And the Lord will grant you plenty of goods, in the fruit of your body, in the increase of your livestock, and in the produce of your ground, in the land of which the Lord swore to your fathers to give you. The Lord will open to you His good treasure, the heavens, to give the rain to your land in its season, and to bless all the work of your hand. You shall lend to many nations, but you shall not borrow. And the Lord will make you the head and not the tail; you shall be above only, and not be beneath, if you heed the commandments of the Lord your God, which I command you today, and are careful to observe them. So you shall not turn aside from any of the words which I command you this day, to the right or the left, to go after other gods to serve them (Deuteronomy 28:1–14).

Carefully notice that in this covenant God hints at a much larger purpose than merely this one nation following their God and receiving His blessings for themselves alone. He promised Abraham that he would be a blessing to all nations (Gentiles) so, here we see that God's larger purpose was so that "all peoples of the earth shall see that you are called by the name of the Lord, and they shall be afraid of you" (v. 10). This was an integral part of being the nation of priests to their God as was the stated purpose for God calling out this nation of Israel.

But now we need to look at the curses that would come upon the nation if they failed to obey the law as God required and the people promised to do. Again, I will quote from Deuteronomy where Moses summarizes the curses for the people shortly before they finally entered the promised land. I would encourage the reader to read the entire chapter on their own, as this is just a summary.

If you do not carefully observe all the words of this law that are written in this book, that you may fear this glorious and awesome name, THE LORD YOUR GOD, then the Lord will bring upon you and your descendants extraordinary plagues — great and prolonged plagues — and serious and prolonged sicknesses. Moreover He will bring back on you all the diseases of Egypt, of which you were afraid, and they shall cling to you. Also every sickness and every plague, which is not written in this Book of the Law, will the Lord bring upon you until you are destroyed. You shall be left few in number, whereas you were as the stars of heaven in multitude, because you would not obey the voice of the Lord your God. And it shall be, that just as the Lord rejoiced over you to do you good and multiply you, so the Lord will rejoice over you to destroy you and bring you to nothing; and you shall be plucked from off the land which you go to possess.

Then the Lord will scatter you among all peoples, from one end of the earth to the other, and there you shall serve other gods, which neither you nor your fathers have known — wood and stone. And among those nations you shall find no rest, nor shall the sole of your foot have a resting place; but there the Lord will give you a trembling heart, failing eyes, and anguish of soul. Your life shall hang in doubt before you; you shall fear day and night, and have no assurance of life. In the morning you shall say, 'Oh, that it were evening!' And at evening you shall say, 'Oh, that it were morning!' because of the fear which terrifies your heart, and because of the sight which your eyes see.

And the Lord will take you back to Egypt in ships, by the way of which I said to you, 'You shall never see it again.' And there you shall be offered for sale to your enemies as male and female slaves, but no one will buy you" (Deuteronomy 28:58–68)

In some ways this might seem harsh to some who do not understand God's larger purpose. It becomes evident as a person studies God's word that God had a specific purpose in mind. When the created spirit that was created in the Image of God died in Adam and Eve, it left a huge void in human nature that mankind has been trying to fill it ever since. Many nations created their own hierarchy of gods to worship and look to in order to fulfill the longing in their souls. God always had a witness in the world that would uphold His standards and walk by faith, but overall, the whole world went astray and could not even understand life or its larger purpose. Consider as an example the Jewish scholar Nicodemus who came to Jesus by night looking for an answer to this very question and Jesus told him that he must be bon-again of the Spirit (John 3: 1–21) in order to understand the answer to the question of God's ultimate purpose for mankind. Consequently, because people continued to ask the question and stumble over answers that came short of providing satisfaction. Paul explains the purpose of this complex, temporary, conditional covenant that became so controversial for the early church. Paul teaches us that "(t)herefore the law was our tutor to bring us to Christ, that we might be justified by faith" (Galatians 3:24). So, the law's purpose was to teach us something about the promised coming Messiah, that all Israel was looking for. Now a tutor is someone who is trained in a particular subject, trade or some skill, and is hired to train another in that subject, trade or skill. In this case it was the knowledge of God. Because of the fallen nature of mankind, they had no ability to understand spiritual realities, and because God is Spirit, they had no understanding of God. Consequently, the law concentrated on teaching them about Him. And as stated earlier, the law concentrates on the one major aspect of who God is. John was clear and specific when he said, "(h)e who does not love does not know God, for God is love" (1 John 4:8). The first 4 commandments concerned our love for God and the last six concerned our love for others. If people could just learn to love, then every other aspect of life would be clear. The fall of mankind changed humankind from God-centered love to self-centered love. Until people learn to love, we will never progress in God's sight.

Teaching people how to love God and their neighbor was the clear purpose of the covenant that God made with Moses and the Children of Israel. But what are we left with when the law comes to its fulfillment? Paul answers that question in the next verses.

> But after faith has come, we are no longer under a tutor.
>
> For you are all sons of God through faith in Christ Jesus. For as many of you as were baptized into Christ have put on Christ. There is neither Jew nor Greek, there is neither slave nor free, there is neither male nor female; for you are all one in Christ Jesus. And if you are Christ's, then you are Abraham's seed, and heirs according to the promise (Galatians 3:25–29).

This does, however, leave one very important question that must be answered. Why, if the law displayed what love is and how love relates to God and one's neighbor, was it temporary? Don't we still need to know and live love's principles today? The answer is also answered by Paul in his letter to the church in Rome.

> There is therefore now no condemnation to those who are in Christ Jesus, who do not walk according to the flesh, but according to the Spirit. For the law of the Spirit of life in Christ Jesus has made me free from the law of sin and death. For what the law could not do in that it was weak through the flesh, God did by sending His own Son in the likeness of sinful flesh, on account of sin: He condemned sin in the flesh, that the righteous requirement of the law might be fulfilled in us who do not walk according to the flesh but according to the Spirit. For those who live according to the flesh set their minds on the things of the flesh, but those who live according

to the Spirit, the things of the Spirit. For to be carnally minded is death, but to be spiritually minded is life and peace. Because the carnal mind is enmity against God; for it is not subject to the law of God, nor indeed can be. So then, those who are in the flesh cannot please God.

But you are not in the flesh but in the Spirit, if indeed the Spirit of God dwells in you. Now if anyone does not have the Spirit of Christ, he is not His. And if Christ is in you, the body is dead because of sin, but the Spirit is life because of righteousness. But if the Spirit of Him who raised Jesus from the dead dwells in you, He who raised Christ from the dead will also give life to your mortal bodies through His Spirit who dwells in you (Romans 8:1–11).

To understand the mandatory presence of the Holy Spirit is very important. The law was given to govern the flesh nature, or as we have called it elsewhere, the fallen nature of mankind, whereas God designed us to be governed by the Spirit. Remember Jesus's conversation with the Jewish scholar, Nicodemus, where Jesus was truly clear that unless one is born-again of the Spirit of God, he/she cannot enter the kingdom or understand spiritual truth. This is Paul's point in verse 3, where he reminds us that "(f)or what the law could not do in that it was weak through the flesh, God did by sending His own Son in the likeness of sinful flesh, on account of sin: He condemned sin in the flesh" (Romans 8:3). The law could never save a person because it was meant to save the flesh as Paul points out for us when he is explaining the difference between faith and flesh. "Yet the law is not of faith, but "the man who does them shall live by them" (Galatians 3:12). In other words, God was using a tutor, the law, to give the people a foundation to prepare them for the time when the Spirit would again be available to them, and then at that time, they would not need the law any longer, but would have the real leader in their lives, the Holy Spirit. Jesus was abundantly clear when He told the disciples, however they did not understand until the Holy Spirit was given to them. Listen to Jesus teach the disciples where their true life came from. "It is the Spirit who gives life; the flesh profits nothing. The words that I speak to you are spirit, and they are life" (John 6:63). The Spirit gives us true life, and the Word of God is only understood and applied to our lives by the Spirit as well. This speaks clearly of the importance of reading, studying, and meditating on the Word of God on a daily basis, but then that is a subject for another day.

So, we must conclude that the covenant God made with Moses and the nation of Israel, the physical descendants of Abraham with whom He made a permanent covenant, that this covenant was conditional and temporary and came to a conclusion when Jesus ascended to the right hand of the Father and sent the Holy Spirit to dwell in those who would believe in the gospel message. And that hopefully is you the reader. Now it is time to move on to the next covenant God made and that is the covenant He made with David.

GOD'S COVENANT WITH DAVID

God's covenant with David is in all reality a renewal of the covenant He made with Abraham, but with added benefits and further explanation of its purpose and plan. We have to keep in mind the fact that a lot of details had to be left out or covered in a thick enough layer of mysticism and symbolism so that God's arch enemy Satan could not find out the details of God's plan of redemption. Therefore, we must dig deep and rely on New Testament revelation and the anointing of the Holy Spirit to see everything that is there. Another element that we have to understand, and can be very confusing, is the fact that "For they are not all Israel who are of Israel," (Romans 9:6). In the chapter on the nature of Christ, we learned that Jesus was all God as well as all human, and therefore we must discern when we are reading in Scripture about Him, whether the writer is talking about Him in His humanity, or in His divinity. We have the same dilemma here. Because not everyone who is born as the physical descendent of Abraham is considered Israel in Scripture, but only those who are in Christ, the promised "seed" of Abraham are the true Israel, and recipients of the conditions of this covenant with David. "That is, those who are the children of the flesh, these are not the children of God; but the children of the promise are counted as the seed" (Romans 9:8). And because it is not always one hundred percent clear which one the author is speaking of, it can be confusing and has led to some controversy within the church and even some division in interpreting and understanding some of the promises.

I will make every effort to make room for some variant understanding. We will examine the conditions and applications of this important eternal covenant God made with David and his "seed". While some have seen up to seven provisions in this covenant, I think it is safe to say that the covenant included three interconnected elements, which are a line of descendants, an eternal throne, and an eternal kingdom looking forward to the reign of his promised "seed" Jesus the Christ of God.

The initial covenant is given to David by the prophet Nathan and contained all three elements mentioned above.

> Now therefore, thus shall you say to My servant David, 'Thus says the Lord of hosts: "I took you from the sheepfold, from following the sheep, to be ruler over My people, over Israel. And I have been with you wherever you have gone, and have cut off all your enemies from before you, and have made you a great name, like the name of the great men who are on the earth. Moreover I will appoint a place for My people Israel, and will plant them, that they may dwell in a place of their own and move no more; nor shall the sons of wickedness oppress them anymore, as previously, since the time that I commanded judges to be over My people Israel, and have caused you to rest from all your enemies. Also the Lord tells you that He will make you a house.
>
> When your days are fulfilled and you rest with your fathers, I will set up your seed after you, who will come from your body, and I will establish his kingdom. He shall build a house for My name, and I will establish the

throne of his kingdom forever. I will be his Father, and
he shall be My son. If he commits iniquity, I will chasten
him with the rod of men and with the blows of the sons of
men. But My mercy shall not depart from him, as I took
it from Saul, whom I removed from before you. And your
house and your kingdom shall be established forever
before you. Your throne shall be established forever"' (2
Samuel 7:8–16).

Notice however that it is "the children of the promise are counted
as the seed" (Romans 9:8b). Nevertheless, we don't learn that until the
New Testament and no one but God understood His plan or the meaning
of his "seed" until after God's plan was fulfilled. It is obvious that even
the disciples of Jesus did not fully understand this truth until several
years into the life of the church when Peter was taught it by going to
Cornelius's house and seeing the Holy Spirit poured out on the Gentiles
the same as it had been on the Jews. "Then Peter opened his mouth and
said: In truth I perceive that God shows no partiality. But in every nation
whoever fears Him and works righteousness is accepted by Him" (Acts
10:34–35). Cornelius was a Gentile and Jews were not to associate with
Gentiles; it took a sovereign act of God to convince Peter to go. But when
he was obedient to God's directive, he was quick to learn and accept the
new revelation. It was only from that experience and revelation of the
Holy Spirit that the church learned that the true "seed" of God's promise
was "whoever believes" and comes to Jesus by faith in His sacrifice for
mankind. We then will look at the provisions with that revelation in
mind.

First, we see it in the Psalms, which is not surprising considering how
close David is associated with the Psalms.

I have made a covenant with My chosen,
I have sworn to My servant David:
'Your seed I will establish forever,
And build up your throne to all generations.'"(Psalm
89:3–4).

And a few verses later in the same Psalm, we read -

> Then You spoke in a vision to Your holy one,
> And said: "I have given help to one who is mighty;
> I have exalted one chosen from the people.
> I have found My servant David;
> With My holy oil I have anointed him,
> With whom My hand shall be established;
> Also My arm shall strengthen him.
> The enemy shall not outwit him,
> Nor the son of wickedness afflict him.
> I will beat down his foes before his face,
> And plague those who hate him.
> But My faithfulness and My mercy shall be with him,
> And in My name his horn shall be exalted.
> Also I will set his hand over the sea,
> And his right hand over the rivers.
> He shall cry to Me, 'You are my Father,
> My God, and the rock of my salvation.'
> Also I will make him My firstborn,
> The highest of the kings of the earth.
> My mercy I will keep for him forever,
> And My covenant shall stand firm with him.
> His seed also I will make to endure forever,
> And his throne as the days of heaven (Psalm 89:19–29).

Notice especially verse 29 where the "seed" is mentioned. This of course, according to New Testament revelation is referring to Christ. So we see the first clue that it is referring to something other-physical. That is, we know that flesh does not live eternally, consequently, we must conclude that it is referring to something else. And of course, that something else, is none other than the second member of the Godhead, the eternal Son of God who became man for redemption's sake or as the writer of Hebrews says, "(b)ut we see Jesus, who was made a little lower than the angels, for the suffering of death crowned with glory and honor, that He, by the grace of God, might taste death for everyone" (Hebrews 2:9). And then, of course, we can't neglect what Isaiah the prophet prophesied about this "seed" of David. Isaiah had a lot to say about the covenant God made with David, but I just want to look at two of them here.

> For unto us a Child is born,
> Unto us a Son is given;
> And the government will be upon His shoulder.
> And His name will be called
> Wonderful, Counselor, Mighty God,
> Everlasting Father, Prince of Peace.
> Of the increase of His government and peace
> There will be no end,
> Upon the throne of David and over His kingdom,
> To order it and establish it with judgment and justice
> From that time forward, even forever.
> The zeal of the Lord of hosts will perform this (Isaiah 9:6–7).

And then, the most quoted verses from Isaiah, speaking directly about not just who the "seed" is, but what His ministry and work would be. And it is important to note that this is the very Scripture Jesus Himself quoted when He identified Himself to the congregation at His home synagogue in Nazareth recorded in Luke 4:18–19 .

> The Spirit of the Lord God is upon Me,
> Because the Lord has anointed Me
> To preach good tidings to the poor;
> He has sent Me to heal the brokenhearted,
> To proclaim liberty to the captives,
> And the opening of the prison to those who are bound;
> To proclaim the acceptable year of the Lord,
> And the day of vengeance of our God;
> To comfort all who mourn,

To console those who mourn in Zion,
To give them beauty for ashes,
The oil of joy for mourning,
The garment of praise for the spirit of heaviness;
That they may be called trees of righteousness,
The planting of the Lord, that He may be glorified"
(Isaiah 61:1–3)

We cannot neglect to mention what Jeremiah the prophet had to say regarding this "seed" of David. For he was given the task of revealing even more information about who this "seed" was and what His purpose and mission would be. Of course, Ezekiel, Hosea, and Amos also gave us some more insight into this covenant and its provisions. First listen to Jeremiah.

Behold, the days are coming," says the Lord,
"That I will raise to David a Branch of righteousness;
A King shall reign and prosper,
And execute judgment and righteousness in the earth.
In His days Judah will be saved,
And Israel will dwell safely;
Now this is His name by which He will be called:
THE LORD OUR RIGHTEOUSNESS (Jeremiah
23:5–6).

And a few chapters later Jeremiah gave this encouraging prophesy.

For it shall come to pass in that day,'
Says the Lord of hosts,
'That I will break his yoke from your neck,
And will burst your bonds;
Foreigners shall no more enslave them.
But they shall serve the Lord their God,
And David their king,
Whom I will raise up for them (Jeremiah 30:8–9).

And the most encouraging promise of all is that this covenant is absolute, will not, indeed cannot be broken.

> Thus says the Lord: 'If you can break My covenant with the day and My covenant with the night, so that there will not be day and night in their season, then My covenant may also be broken with David My servant, so that he shall not have a son to reign on his throne, and with the Levites, the priests, My ministers. As the host of heaven cannot be numbered, nor the sand of the sea measured, so will I multiply the descendants of David My servant and the Levites who minister to Me' (Jeremiah 33:20–22).

While there is probably a lot more that could be said about this covenant that God made with David, I believe that this should prove beyond any doubt that Christ is the ultimate "son of David" and the ultimate recipient of the throne of David. "He will be great, and will be called the Son of the Highest; and the Lord God will give Him the throne of His father David" (Luke 1:32). And He is also the ultimate ruler of the Davidic kingdom. "And He will reign over the house of Jacob forever, and of His kingdom there will be no end" (Luke 1:33).

As we wrap up our discussion of the Covenant God made with David, we need to realize that it is an extension and expansion of the covenant God made with Abraham. And remember that that covenant was made by God alone as He put Abraham to sleep and signed the covenant by Himself, swearing to fulfill the covenant without requiring anything from Abraham or His seed. All that is required to receive all the benefits and provisions of that covenant is to simply accept it as Abraham did. Remember Abraham believed God and God counted it to him as righteousness (Galatians 3:6), the one thing needed to enter into God's presence. "But without faith it is impossible to please Him, for he who comes to God must believe that He is, and that He is a rewarder of those who diligently seek Him" (Hebrews 11:6). A simple formula, that when followed, will have eternal rewards. And now we need to examine the final covenant, referred to as the New Covenant.

GOD'S NEW COVENANT

I could easily just copy what was said about the covenants with Abraham and David and paste it here to explain the new covenant. However, because it was hidden deeply in the Old Testament, and because it was not revealed until Jesus was sacrificed and hung on the cross, buried for three days, raised from the dead and ascended to the right hand of God, and sent His Holy Spirit to teach and reveal all things to His people, no one could see it or understand it. Its revelation was a slow progressive unveiling and generally happened by experience. Consequently, to make sure that it is absolutely clear to each reader, I will begin at the beginning with it being prophesied by the prophet Jeremiah all the way through the Scripture. I trust the reader has paid close attention to the sections of this chapter on the covenant with Abraham as well as the covenant with David, because I will refer to provisions contained within them. An understanding of these two covenants will be necessary to fully understand this new covenant.

We need to begin with the promise of a new covenant given by Jeremiah the prophet.

> Behold, the days are coming, says the Lord, when I will make a new covenant with the house of Israel and with the house of Judah — not according to the covenant that I made with their fathers in the day that I took them by the hand to lead them out of the land of Egypt, My covenant which they broke, though I was a husband to them, says the Lord. But this is the covenant that I will make with the house of Israel after those days, says the Lord: I will put My law in their minds, and write it on their hearts; and I will be their God, and they shall be My people. No more shall every man teach his neighbor, and every man his brother, saying, 'Know the Lord,' for they all shall know Me, from the least of them to the greatest of them, says the Lord. For I will forgive their iniquity, and their sin I will remember no more" (Jeremiah 31:31–34).

Notice first that the prophet emphasizes the fact that it will be different than the covenant that Israel has known, ("not according to the covenant I made with their fathers"). They are living under and being judged by the covenant of Moses, which is the law, and a temporary conditional covenant. Notice as well, an important difference that is revealed. Whereas the covenant that they were living under had the law engraved on tablets of stone and explained on scrolls emphasizing the conditions of the law, this new covenant "will put My law in their minds, and write it on their hearts" (v. 33b). We know today that He was speaking of the Holy Spirit who would be sent after Jesus's ascension into heaven. And further, everyone who is born-again of the Spirit would know God because they could now experience His presence and have their sins forgiven.

We don't hear much more about this new covenant until we hear Jesus revealing it to His disciples at the last supper before He was betrayed into the hands of those who would execute Him. Matthew, Mark and Luke all record His words to them,

> Then He took the cup, and gave thanks, and gave it to them, saying, "Drink from it, all of you. For this is My blood of the new covenant, which is shed for many for the remission of sins. But I say to you, I will not drink of this fruit of the vine from now on until that day when I drink it new with you in My Father's kingdom" (Matthew 26:27–29).

And Paul recites these words to the church in Corinth to encourage them to remember His words by celebrating a ceremony regularly. "In the same manner He also took the cup after supper, saying, "This cup is the new covenant in My blood. This do, as often as you drink it, in remembrance of Me" (1 Corinthians 11:25).

The stated purpose is to help the church remember the terms of this covenant. If it is worth instituting a religious ritual to ensure that the people remember it, then it must be an important covenant. Therefore, we need to give more effort to understand it so we can remember it accurately as we celebrate it on a regular basis. The New Testament church celebrates what most call communion or the Lord's supper, but one has to ask a serious question; "Do we really understand what we are celebrating?" I believe that is an important question to ask because millions of people celebrate Christmas every year, and yet most do not stop and remember accurately what the day represents. A day when God Himself, humbled Himself and took on the form of a man "He humbled Himself and became obedient to the point of death, even the death of the cross" (Philippians 2:9). It is therefore vital for Christians today, when they participate in the ritual of communion, to stop, reflect, and truly remember that they are in fact celebrating that God actually died for their sins and they are truly free from the requirements of the law and are under the new covenant that God made with them, through Abraham, David, and Jesus Christ. They are truly free to serve and worship Him in spirit and in truth.

Finally, the unknown writer of Hebrews picks up the theme and explains it further. The author begins his/her discussion by quoting from the prophet Jeremiah that we quoted above, where Jeremiah introduced us to the idea of a new covenant. But he says this about the new covenant; "In that He says, "A new covenant," He has made the first obsolete. Now what is becoming obsolete and growing old is ready to vanish away" (Hebrews 8:13). The writer then continues by explaining some of the rituals from the first covenant of law and why they were now "obsolete". I need to remind you of an important truth here, because, while it is true that the covenant that he is referring to here was growing old and ready to vanish away, it was actually introduced to Moses and the nation of Israel at least four centuries after the first terms of this "new covenant" were introduced to Abraham. As well listen to what Paul said about it in Galatians chapter 3,

> And this I say, that the law, which was four hundred and thirty years later, cannot annul the covenant that was confirmed before by God in Christ, that it should make the promise of no effect. For if the inheritance is of the law, it is no longer of promise; but God gave it to Abraham by promise (vv 17–18).

So, while the writer of Hebrews refers to the covenant with Abraham as the new covenant, it was in all reality the temporary, conditional covenant, or the "tutor" that was designed to bring God's people to know Him that was growing old and ready to vanish. So, it was new to Israel, and it was the second one that God made with Israel (the first through Abraham and the second through Moses). Nevertheless, it was the first and only unconditional and eternal covenant that God made with mankind. But when understood in its context, the writer of Hebrews was writing to Jews and about Jews who would have known the law and that is the only covenant that they would have been familiar with. But for the Gentiles, this was the first and only covenant He made with them as included in the covenant with Abraham when God promised him that he would be a blessing to all nations. "And in you all the families of the earth shall be blessed" (Genesis 12:3b).

Now I probably need to pause here and acknowledge that there are some Bible teachers who see two covenants contained in this "new covenant". The controversy is over the distinction between the Jews and the Gentiles and some of the provisions of the covenant that appear to be only for the physical descendants of Abraham. In other words, is God making one covenant with the physical nation of Israel and another with Gentiles? I don't have space in this book to explore the whole controversy, however, since it does affect how one views the application of this covenant, we have to at least mention it. The division involves some of the terms of the covenant made with Abraham. If we only rely on the Old Testament revelation, it would be easy to come to the conclusion that God elected the physical descendants of Abraham for certain blessings and special treatment. However, when one considers New Testament revelation, it is much more difficult to come to that certain conclusion.

The Jewish leaders of the early church, who were all Jews, had to face the controversy early in the history of the church. The Jews assumed at first that salvation through Jesus Christ was only for the Jews. But then with Peter, and his experience with Cornelius and God obviously welcoming the Gentiles into the church, the Jewish leaders then, for the most part, began to think that the new covenant was for Jews and Gentiles alike, however, the Gentiles had to obey the law of the covenant with

Moses in order to become part of the new spiritual Israel. Nevertheless, we notice an interesting thing that seemed to accompany this debate. First the church leaders called the first church council, recorded for us in Acts 15, to discuss the matter and came to the conclusion that Gentiles did not need to obey the law but only a few provisions that had to do with some foods and sexual behavior. That only settled the issue for Gentiles because we see Jews still insisting on following the law of Moses. We even see Paul, when he went back to visit Jerusalem to visit the leaders there, that he seemed to believe that Jews should follow the law of Moses because we see him obeying the law for purification and not allowing Gentiles into the temple, as well as other behaviors that the law dictated. This trip is recorded for us in Acts 21 and could all by itself indicate that Jews indeed had to still obey the law of Moses under the new covenant.

That seems to become a strong argument for the doctrine of two strands to this new covenant that Jeremiah prophesied about. Nevertheless, there are also strong arguments for the new covenant being one covenant for all of mankind with God not making any distinction between the two camps. For example, consider the parable of the wild olive tree being grafted into the domestic olive tree. I will have to use a rather long portion of Scripture to make this important point, but because this is not a new question, but an ancient question as old as the church itself, I want to quote from Paul's letter to the Romans.

> For if the firstfruit is holy, the lump is also holy; and if the root is holy, so are the branches. And if some of the branches were broken off, and you, being a wild olive tree, were grafted in among them, and with them became a partaker of the root and fatness of the olive tree, do not boast against the branches. But if you do boast, remember that you do not support the root, but the root supports you.
>
> You will say then, "Branches were broken off that I might be grafted in." Well said. Because of unbelief they were broken off, and you stand by faith. Do not be haughty,

but fear. For if God did not spare the natural branches, He may not spare you either. Therefore consider the goodness and severity of God: on those who fell, severity; but toward you, goodness, if you continue in His goodness. Otherwise you also will be cut off. And they also, if they do not continue in unbelief, will be grafted in, for God is able to graft them in again. For if you were cut out of the olive tree which is wild by nature, and were grafted contrary to nature into a cultivated olive tree, how much more will these, who are natural branches, be grafted into their own olive tree?

For I do not desire, brethren, that you should be ignorant of this mystery, lest you should be wise in your own opinion, that blindness in part has happened to Israel until the fullness of the Gentiles has come in. And so all Israel will be saved, as it is written:

> "The Deliverer will come out of Zion,
>
> And He will turn away ungodliness from Jacob;
>
> For this is My covenant with them,
>
> When I take away their sins."

Concerning the gospel they are enemies for your sake, but concerning the election they are beloved for the sake of the fathers. For the gifts and the calling of God are irrevocable. For as you were once disobedient to God, yet have now obtained mercy through their disobedience, even so these also have now been disobedient, that through the mercy shown you they also may obtain

mercy. For God has committed them all to disobedience,
that He might have mercy on all (Romans 11:16–32).

So now we need to look closely at what Paul is teaching. Remember
that at this time in Rome the church was under severe persecution and
there were both Jews and Gentile members of the church, although, it
appears that about this same time many of the Jews had been expelled
from Rome by the Roman government (see Acts 18:2). Consequently,
it is almost certain that this same controversy plagued the church there
and Paul was addressing a real problem that existed in the church. Notice
Paul's first argument in verse 18, "remember that you do not support the
root, but the root supports you." In other words, both the wild olive tree
branches and the domestic olive tree branches had been grafted into one
tree stump, both support by the same root system of the domestic olive
tree. Then Paul teaches that it was because of unbelief that these domestic
olive tree branches (the Jews, the physical descendants of Abraham)
were broken off from the support of the root system, but "if they do not
continue in unbelief, will be grafted in, for God is able to graft them in
again" (v. 23).

Then Paul makes an interesting observation. He said, "(f)or I do
not desire, brethren, that you should be ignorant of this mystery, lest
you should be wise in your own opinion (v. 25). This is where most
controversies come from, pride in our own opinion, as James so aptly
points out in James 4:1. Paul concludes this argument with the conclusion
that because "the gifts and the calling of God are irrevocable" (v. 29), the
Jews will be given another chance to be grafted back into the domestic
olive tree from which they were broken off. But, consider carefully
Paul's point in this whole argument. The Jews were broken off from the
domestic olive tree and will be grafted back into the same tree, whereas
the Gentiles were grafted into a completely different kind of tree than the
one which they were broken off. So we Gentiles cannot boast that we have
replaced the Jews as God's favored people, we have simple been invited
to join them in their rightful place.

But there is another portion of Scripture that speaks even more clearly
about this supposed division between Jews and Gentiles. Because as I said

earlier, this strong wall between Jews and Gentiles had been firmly in place since God led the nation of Israel out of Egypt, and commanded Israel to separate themselves from any contact with Gentiles, except to do business with them. Remember, the woman at the well understood that Jews don't associate with Gentiles when "the woman of Samaria said to Him, "How is it that You, being a Jew, ask a drink from me, a Samaritan woman?" For Jews have no dealings with Samaritans" (John 4:9). And many Jews of the New Testament church still thought this way. Therefore, Paul addressed this controversary head on when he wrote to the church at Ephesus.

> For He Himself is our peace, who has made both one, and has broken down the middle wall of separation, having abolished in His flesh the enmity, that is, the law of commandments contained in ordinances, so as to create in Himself one new man from the two, thus making peace, and that He might reconcile them both to God in one body through the cross, thereby putting to death the enmity. And He came and preached peace to you who were afar off and to those who were near (Ephesians 2:14–17).

While there still remains some confusion over the issue, it seems fairly clear that God intended from the very beginning to provide redemption for "whosoever will" (Revelation 22:17 KJV) believe and obey, He did it over many centuries and a little at a time as humans could understand it and He could find faithful men and women who would believe Him as Noah, Abraham, Moses, David and Jesus did providing a way out of the death Adam and Eve brought to all humankind at their fall. God was able to do that through Jesus, the Christ of God "(f)or God so loved the world that He gave His only begotten Son, that whoever believes in Him should not perish but have everlasting life. For God did not send His Son into the world to condemn the world, but that the world through Him might be saved" (John 3:16–17).

To wrap up this chapter on the covenants of God, it seems fitting to remember that our God, the Father of our Lord Jesus Christ, and giver of His Holy Spirit is the same yesterday, today and forever (Hebrews 13:8), and therefore His plans and purposes have not changed since He first devised them with all three members of the Godhead active in them. Therefore, the desire to have His highest creation, created in His own image, partake of every tree of the Garden, with the one exception of the Tree of the Knowledge of Good and Evil remains. These covenants were all entered into with the one goal in mind, and that is to restore mankind to his and her original state and then put them back on the path He desired for them in the first place. God's goal does not stop when He returns and puts us in a new heaven and earth that Isaiah the prophet first spoke about and Peter affirmed was God's goal.

> "For behold, I create new heavens and a new earth; And the former shall not be remembered or come to mind" (Isaiah 65:17).

And Peter says,

> "Nevertheless we, according to His promise, look for new heavens and a new earth in which righteousness dwells" (2 Peter 3:13).

Understand that God did not create all of creation and put a man and woman in charge of it all so they could sit in a rocking chair and watch it throughout eternity. He intended them to tend His garden and care for it and did not intend that work be a chore but rather a pleasure and a source whereby to exercise their creative abilities with what God gave them. That remains His goal, to have mankind living in His Paradise, working in it, partaking of the Tree of Life and living and enjoying Him and one another forever.

My goal for the reader is that they might accept God's offer of salvation and restoration and then when you do, to share it with as many people as God might send your way.

6

WHAT DOES IT MEAN
TO BE A CHRISTIAN?

THE DIFFERENCE BETWEEN
BELIEVER AND UNBELIEVER

There are literally hundreds of opinions of what it means to be a Christian, but, like any other doctrine, we must turn to Scripture to get a clear revelation of what God expects of those who claim to be following Christ. And it would seem appropriate to find the first time we even find this term used in Scripture.

> Then Barnabas departed for Tarsus to seek Saul. And when he had found him, he brought him to Antioch. So it was that for a whole year they assembled with the church and taught a great many people. And the disciples were first called Christians in Antioch (Acts 11:25–26).

What does it mean to be a Christian? While I could go a number of different directions in answering this question, I want to focus on the changes and the lifestyle of such a person who holds the title "Christian". The reason I want to go from that position is because when the disciples in Antioch were first called "Christian" it was because of their lifestyle and witness, rather than some title that someone chose for the group.

A Christian, first of all, is a person who has put their total trust in Jesus Christ and has decided to follow Him no matter what. Now here one must also take into consideration Jesus's words on the subject when He told a parable on four different types of soil (a parable recorded in three of the four gospels, Matthew 13:3ff; Mark 4ff; and Luke 8:5ff). Three of the four soils did not produce any fruit and therefore did not make it to the end. Now the question becomes, were they saved, and if so, what happened to them when they fell away. And if they were not saved, why did they begin? In other words, are we secure in Christ or does our salvation depend on our works? Of course, anyone who has studied theology or church History at all will know that this is one of the most hotly debated topics in all Christendom. Once a person is saved, can he/she loose that salvation or are they secure for all eternity?

The second thing that has to be discussed is what does salvation consist of. Does it consist of our work and our decisions, or does it depend solely on God's choice and actions on our behalf. That, of course, has been the discussion since Christians were first called Christians in Antioch. It would seem that the discussion would require us to reread and try to understand the promise God made to Abraham and His "seed" which Paul is very clear that this "seed" is Christ. Paul is just as clear that the covenant God made with Abraham is the permanent covenant that Christians can rightly claim today, while the law was a temporary covenant that lasted only until the covenant with Abraham was fulfilled in Christ's birth, death, resurrection, and ascension. So those who are born again and in Christ would fall under the covenant with Abraham that passed through King David and then on to Jesus, known as the Christ of God and through Him to those who believe in Him and are born again of His Spirit.

Now, as we go back to the covenant with Abraham, we see clearly that God was not going to take any chances whatsoever this time. Remember at initial creation when He made a spirit for mankind that was first of all a created spirit that, while in the very image of God, was given on a conditional promise that as that if they were to partake of that tree of the Knowledge of Good and Evil, they would die.

We all know the sad story that they did, in fact partake of the tree and did die spiritually while their soul was corrupted with total wickedness and their bodies began the slow process of death, sickness and disease (see the full examination of creation in Chapter 1). But we find out immediately that God already knew what their choices would be, so He devised a plan to redeem the crown jewel of His creation. Now we fast forward to Abraham where we witness God begin to actually flesh out that plan of salvation. It is important that we look very closely at this promise of God because that is the promise that we live under today as disciples of Jesus Christ. God was not willing to take a chance or only make a conditional promise again, but rather He decided to make a promise that would not and could not change because it came from the very heart of God. Therefore, as we study this covenant closely, we find a few very clear marks of God's sovereignty all over it. First, God tested Abraham to be sure that he was trustworthy and would obey God so the covenant could be established for Him and His "seed" after Him. This is why God had Abraham perform the typical cultural ritual of a normal legal contract for His day and culture that Abraham would know and understand. So, Abraham took three animals and two birds and killed them, split the animal's apart and laid half on one side and the other half on the other side with a path down the center with one whole dead bird on each side as well (see Genesis 15:9–11).

Now the standard practice of making a covenant in that day was to kill an animal or animals and after cutting them in two and laying them on the ground with the two halves of the animals apart with a narrow path between the halves. The two people involved in the contract would then walk down the center between the halves of the dead mutilated animals and while they walked down the center they would both call out curses on themselves essentially saying, "May the same thing happen to me as has happened to these animals if I should break any part of this contract". The specific provisions of the contract were written out and what we call a notary public would witness the contract as both parties signed that they understood and agreed to the provisions of the contract. In Abraham's culture witnesses would watch as both parties walked between the pieces swearing to fulfill the requirements of the contract.

Notice what God did after Abraham killed the animals and the birds. God then put Abraham to sleep, and Abraham simply watched as God Himself walked down the center of those dead animals swearing to uphold the provisions of the contract and Scripture notes that "For when God made a promise to Abraham, because He could swear by no one greater, He swore by Himself" (Hebrews 6:13).

In other words, the new covenant is a one-sided covenant, as it were, with God Himself taking on the full responsibility of keeping the covenant with Abraham (us) having no part whatsoever except believing it and accepting it and then appropriating it to ourselves. Remember, the first promise to Adam and Eve was conditional and depended on them obeying God's command to not eat of the fruit of the forbidden tree. The covenant He made with Israel at Sinai was conditional on them keeping all the provisions of the law. However, this promise He made with Abraham was completely unconditional on any human being and only dependent on God's grace and mercy.

Now we must contemplate what all this means for us today. If we would miss the point of this contract, we will miss the entire point of God sending Jesus to earth as a man to die for our sins. The fact of the matter is that a contract is always between two or more people, but this covenant, while it is certainly between two people, the implications are for all eternity between God and everyone who chooses to believe it and accept it. In other words, when I accept Jesus Christ as my personal Lord and Savior, I am initiated into a special group of people known as Christians, or as Scripture puts it, the Body of Christ (referred as such by Paul in 1 Corinthians 12:27 and Ephesians 4:12). This is why Jesus taught Nicodemus the necessity of being baptized in the Holy Spirit, and why He made such statements as we must abide in the vine to have life and to bring forth any kind of fruit. It is very difficult for us humans to accept something for nothing. It seems to grate against our human nature of pride and wanting to receive wages for our work. But when someone simply gives us something, we must first of all, choose to either accept it or reject it. Someone can offer me a free gift, but if I refuse it, it never becomes useful to me nor is it ever my possession. But if I take it, and discover through questioning, research, or being taught by the giver how to use it, and then actually do use it, then I have all the benefits that

that gift has to offer, along with all the responsibility of maintaining it so it remains useful. While I am responsible for what I do with the gift, I can never take credit for buying it, earning it, or even asking for it. I was chosen to receive the gift; however, I do have the responsibility of saying yes or no. God never forces His gift on anyone.

So now we must continue and further explore together what this all means for us today. In other words, now that we have been offered a gift that was purchased by Jesus Christ, and for free for the asking, what does it all mean and what are the implications and responsibilities we have now?

For starters, we must clearly understand the characteristics of the One who gave us the gift. Because Scripture records that God is the same yesterday, today and forever, we can find out His characteristics from Scripture because we will then know what to expect from Him today. And while I will spend some time in proving it to you, I want to say up front that we as born-again Christians are absolutely secure in Christ. There is nothing, anything or anybody, that can separate us from Him and His love for us. He bought us with a steep price, far above what anyone could ever imagine, and He will never let us out of His hand. Like a mother hen who hides her young under her wing and will literally give up her life to protect her young, so God hides us in His hand and has literally given His life to keep us safe and secure. But now we need to look more specifically at what Scripture says about our security in Christ.

THE BELIEVERS SECURITY IN CHRIST

It is sometimes difficult to know exactly where to start a discussion, especially when writing a book because there is so much diversity in readers. Some might be rather new to Christianity while others have been Christians all their lives. On the other hand, not everyone who calls themselves Christian is as enthusiastic, as evident from Jesus's story of the four soils, which means that not every Christian gives themselves equally to reading and studying the Word of God. Therefore, I want to start, just as I did in Chapter 1, at the beginning. In the beginning of God's dealings with His chosen people, Israel, God treated His people differently. For example, listen to God speaking to Moses concerning how He (God) sees the Israelites as distinct and different than the Egyptians; "But against none of the children of Israel shall a dog move its tongue, against man or beast, that you may know that the Lord does make a difference between the Egyptians and Israel" (Exodus 11:7). Understand that He said this while Israel was still in Egypt and just before the last plague where the first-born of both man and beast was to be killed. In other words, God makes a sharp distinction between His people and unbelievers.

This is why God made such a distinction between the covenant He made with Abraham and the covenant He made with Israel as a nation at Sinai. He went to extremes to make the covenant with Abraham unconditional, while the covenant He made with Adam and Eve was conditional, as well as the covenant He made with the nation of Israel that was conditional on them keeping the Law. Pay close attention to the words of Scripture as the writers show clearly that God still makes a sharp distinction between His people, who we call Christians, as opposed to all unbelievers who refuse to accept the covenant Jesus came to secure for those who choose to believe.

For this particular subject I will follow the general outline of a sermon I preached on the subject in the Philippines back in 2016. I came to these conclusions rather recently in my walk with the Lord because at best it is a hard subject and one that has drawn a lot of division among theologians over the centuries. Today the church is about evenly split between what are called Armenians and Calvinists. In other words, for those who might not understand those labels, it simply describes two major camps within the church. Armenians generally believe that once a person is saved and born of the Spirit of God, if they sin, or choose to live in sin, they would argue that that person can, and probably will, lose their salvation. In the other camp known as the Calvinists, they generally believe that if a person is truly born again of the Spirit of God, then it is impossible for them to lose their salvation.

Now I have to reveal that I was raised in a very fundamentalist church, that tried to obey the Old Testament to the letter and even added a few laws and regulations of their own. They believed that if a person was saved, and some would even argue that it was generally impossible for one to know for certain if they were saved before the great White Throne Judgment (Revelation 20:11ff), if that person were to commit any type of sin, and should die before they had time to repent of it, they would go to hell. In fact, I remember one time when my mother was driving with a car full of young kids and was distracted enough that she drove through a stop sign. When someone honked the horn and yelled obscenities at her for running the stop sign, she realized her mistake. She immediately pulled to the side of the road and confessed her sin asking for forgiveness, because she believed that if she should die without confessing and repenting for it, she would go to hell. I was raised with such beliefs and I never really questioned them even as an adult. I did modify them to some degree because when I walked away from the Lord at age 18 and quit going to church and started smoking cigarettes, I convinced myself that the "sins" I was doing were not really that bad so I was all right if I would just ask the Lord to forgive me on rare occasions and "try" to quit.

However, in my late 50's I really began to question these beliefs and began a prayerful investigation. What raised the question to the forefront in my mind was the death of my first wife. She died of cancer at only 52 years of age, and she had smoked cigarettes since the age of 14, so because of my belief that one could lose their salvation if they had unconfessed sin, I began a serious inquiry of God as to her eternal destiny, for she had a cigarette within a half hour of her death and I know that she did not repent of it. The Lord was faithful to give me undeniable proof that she was indeed saved and with Him in heaven, which in turn prompted me to inquire about the security of the believer. God did, in fact, answer me and showed me the truth, but it took a number of years before I finally took the plunge and wrote my first sermon on the subject in 2016 while working as a missionary in the Philippines. While there are many verses that speak on the subject in Scripture, Paul's letter to the Roman church explains his position on the subject best. I want to look at this passage of Scripture in depth because it is here that the Apostle Paul addresses the issue of the believer's security in Christ head-on.

What then shall we say to these things? If God is for us, who can be against us? He who did not spare His own Son, but delivered Him up for us all, how shall He not with Him also freely give us all things? Who shall bring a charge against God's elect? It is God who justifies. Who is he who condemns? It is Christ who died, and furthermore is also risen, who is even at the right hand of God, who also makes intercession for us. Who shall separate us from the love of Christ? Shall tribulation, or distress, or persecution, or famine, or nakedness, or peril, or sword? As it is written:

"For Your sake we are killed all day long; We are accounted as sheep for the slaughter."

Yet in all these things we are more than conquerors through Him who loved us. For I am persuaded that neither death nor life, nor angels nor principalities nor powers, nor things present nor things to come, nor height nor depth, nor any other created thing, shall be able to separate us from the love of God which is in Christ Jesus our Lord" (Romans 8:31–39).

It has been said that it is not *what* you know that matters, but *who* you know. In other words, who is in your corner? Who are your allies that you can rely on to help you? For Christians, the answer is God! The NKJV reads "If God is for us..." but the Greek leaves no uncertainty. A more accurate translation would be "[Since] God is for us..."

The fact of the matter is, He is on our side!

I remember as a young man watching Perry Mason on TV and later Matlock began showing his legal brilliance in the courtroom. Today we have such shows as Law and Order or CSI. However, from my perspective, contained in Scripture is the greatest courtroom drama there ever was or ever will be! Let me be creative for a moment as I envision this scene in God's courtroom. The judge is none other than our Lord Jesus Christ.

The defendant is you and all of humanity. Naturally we don't know what happened in the heavenly realm between Satan and God but allow me to imagine a possibility. The first witness to take the stand is the Law that testifies to the judge that it is obvious that the defendant has done so many of the things that God clearly said one should not do. He would probably mention things list lust and greed and malcontent and the arrogant pride that has shown up so many times. He would further claim that not only were the things God clearly forbid done, but many of the things that He commanded were left undone. He might continue claiming that the defendant did none of what God said should be done like loving others, giving generously, or gladly hearing God's Word. In fact, he could claim that there are literally millions of infractions. The defendant is clearly guilty he would conclude. And of course, the judge would have to ask you if these accusations were true. And you would have no choice but to answer that yes, it is all true. Next death would probably step up and remind the judge what the wage for sin is. He would remind Him that God Himself said that the soul that sins should die. Consequently, he would conclude that the sentence is obvious. This sinner belongs in hell.

Well, I can imagine that the case appears airtight. All the evidence is clearly against you and you find yourself sitting there knowing you have no answer. Death and hell are your certain fate. But then, to your amazement, rather than pound the gavel down and pronounce you guilty, the judge gets up from behind his bench and walks around to your side. You can hardly believe what is happening because God will now serve as your defense attorney! And as we continue to imagine this conversation you hear Him say that although you have failed to live a perfect life of love, He has done that in your place. Even though you have sinned He has paid for that sin with His own life. He acknowledges that you obviously deserve hell, but He has already paid the penalty of hell that you deserve. He goes back behind the bench, pounds the gavel down and pronounces you innocent of all charges as He dismisses the case![20] While this conversation is hypothetical, I believe Scripture would support it.

---

[20] The outline for this hypothetical courtroom drama was suggested by a sermon I read by Pastor Rob Guenther, pastor at Grace Lutheran Church in Kenai, Alaska (used by permission)

> Who will bring any charge against those whom God has
> chosen? It is God who justifies. Who is he that condemns?
> Christ Jesus, who died—more than that, who was raised
> to life—is at the right hand of God and is also interceding
> for us. (Romans 8:33–34)

I believe that now no one can bring any accusation against a truly born-again Christian. We stand innocent before God! Heaven itself is our absolute reward! And that alone brings us true and lasting security.

I read a story somewhere, I do not know if it is true or not, of how the devil approached Martin Luther one day to accuse him. He presented the Reformer with a long list of sins of which he was guilty. When he had finished reading, Luther said to Satan, "Think a little harder; you must have forgotten some." The devil thought a little more and added even more sins to the list. When the devil was done listing all he could think of, Luther simply said, "That's fine. Now write across that list in red ink, "The blood of Jesus Christ, His Son, cleanses us from all sin..." (1 John 1:7b). There was nothing the devil could do except to walk away.

No one can accuse you either, if you are saved by the blood of our Lord Jesus Christ, the devil has nothing on you. The law no longer holds you under its foot. And your conscience itself, must shut up in the face of this rebuttal: "The blood of Jesus Christ, His Son, cleanses us from all sin..." (1 John 1:7b). You are secure in Christ!

Not only is there absolutely no accusation that can be brought against you, but the second point Paul made is that there is no possible separation from Christ

Now some people think "Heaven is mine". And that's probably good and all, but what does God's promise have to do with my life right now? Many people assume that Christianity is a religion for the hereafter, sort of like fire insurance that only pays after a fire, with nothing to do with life here and now. But that could not be further from the truth. You are secure for eternity because there is **no possible accusation** against you, but you are also secure right now, because there is **no possible separation** from the love of Christ!

Now please don't misunderstand me here. God does NOT promise that everything in this life will be pleasant and fun. Quite to the contrary, suffering is assumed when Paul asks, "Who shall separate us from the love of Christ? Shall trouble or hardship or persecution or famine or nakedness or danger or sword?" (Romans 8:35). And he quotes Psalm 44:22 to show that these things should be expected: "As it is written: "For your sake we face death all day long; we are considered as sheep to be slaughtered."

But he answers his own rhetorical questions when he says,

No, in all these things we are more than conquerors through him who loved us. For I am convinced that neither death nor life, neither angels nor demons, neither the present nor the future, nor any powers, neither height nor depth, nor anything else in all creation, will be able to separate us from the love of God that is in Christ Jesus our Lord. (Romans 8:37–39 NIV)[21]

Literally "We are Super-conquerors." We conquer and then some! Why? Not because of our strength or abilities, but through Him who loved us—because nothing will ever "be able to separate us from the love of God that is in Christ Jesus our Lord."

How fortunate we are that nothing can ever separate us from the love of Christ. No matter what type of personal tragedy strikes—sickness or disease, financial struggles or disasters, terrorists or crooks, our own stupid mistakes, no matter what! Nothing can dissolve the bond of love God has created with us. God is always right there with us, upholding us especially through those difficult times. And this security that we have every day should and can change the way we live. We can live in freedom with the certain promise that He will never leave us nor will he ever forsake us. We can live with bold courage as we live for him.

I heard a story some years ago that illustrates the value of security. During the first part of the construction of the Golden Gate Bridge in San Francisco, no safety devices were used, and 23 men fell to their deaths.

---

[21] New International Version, 1978, 1999, International Bible Society.

For the last part of the project, however, a large net costing $100,000 was employed (which back then was a whole lot of money). At least 10 men fell into it and their lives were saved. But an interesting sidelight is the fact that 25 percent more work was accomplished when the men were assured of their safety.

And if you are not yet convinced consider this from the apostle Paul: "But if the Spirit of Him who raised Jesus from the dead dwells in you, He who raised Christ from the dead will also give life to your mortal bodies through His Spirit who dwells in you" (Romans 8:11). The first spirit made in the image of God was a created spirit that came with the warning that if they disobeyed and ate of the tree of the Knowledge of Good and Evil, they would die. And they did in fact die, BUT, God did not take any chances this time. For God so loved His fallen creation that He gave His one and only Son – And His Son when he had laid down His life for our sins, arose from the dead and ascended to the right hand of God, and sent His Spirit to dwell in us and that Spirit is not given with a warning. And that Spirit who is God Himself, cannot die! Therefore, when we are born-again of the Spirit of God, we are absolutely secure in Christ and can rest assured that we will live eternally with Him. "But against none of the children of Israel shall a dog move its tongue, against man or beast, that you may know that the Lord does make a difference between the Egyptians and Israel." (Exodus 11:7). And of course, I pray you understand that all born-again believers are the Israel of God (Galatians 6:16).

CHRISTIANS AS KINGS AND PRIESTS

My son Josiah likes to save "the best for last". Whenever he eats a food that he particularly enjoys, he always scrapes his favorite part to the side and eats everything else first then when he is finished eating that, he will turn to his favorite and slowly enjoy it. I have done about the same thing here. In any discussion of what it means to be a Christian in this world, there are several things that have to be considered. Of course, one has to understand what it means to him or herself and the inner life and thoughts that are involved. Then one needs to clearly understand what it means in our daily life with other members of society; what it means for one's actions and decisions in everyday life; what it means for our conduct and behavior in the body of believers, the church. But I believe the most important aspect of what it means to be a Christian, is the question of "to what end?" In other words, what is my purpose in God's grand design of things. What is my purpose for being alive, for being called to live and work in a particular time and place? So that is how I want to conclude this chapter – discussing why we are on this earth and what should occupy our time and efforts while we are here as born-again sons and daughters of the Lord God Almighty, Father of our Savior, Jesus Christ.

To start, we need to go back to the Old Testament and see what God's purpose was in calling out a people to Himself and why He specifically said, "But against none of the children of Israel shall a dog move its tongue, against man or beast, that you may know that the Lord does make a difference between the Egyptians and Israel" (Exodus 11:7–8). God specifically called out a particular family and gave them a specific assignment. Pay close attention to God's words to Moses as He was instructing Moses on how to lead this great nation out of Egypt and into the Promised Land to fulfill His special purpose for them.

> And Moses went up to God, and the Lord called to him from the mountain, saying, "Thus you shall say to the house of Jacob, and tell the children of Israel: 'You have seen what I did to the Egyptians, and how I bore you on eagles' wings and brought you to Myself. Now therefore, if you will indeed obey My voice and keep My covenant, then you shall be a special treasure to Me above all people; for all the earth is Mine. And you shall be to Me a kingdom of priests and a holy nation.' These are the words which you shall speak to the children of Israel" (Exodus 19:3–6).

Peter tells us that we are "living stones, (are) being built up a spiritual house, a holy priesthood, to offer up spiritual sacrifices acceptable to God through Jesus Christ" (1 Peter 2:5). And he then continues to explain further in verse 9,

> But you are a chosen generation, a royal priesthood, a holy nation, His own special people, that you may proclaim the praises of Him who called you out of darkness into His marvelous light; 10 who once were not a people but are now the people of God, who had not obtained mercy but now have obtained mercy.

Now, I realize that some of you will say "I thought the priesthood and the sacrificial system were done away with in Christ". So, what is Peter talking about? Note however, that this is a universal call, not simply for some specific group of people. Note as well that he references a group of people that "were not a people but are now the people of God" (1 Peter 2:10). So, he is obviously referring to the church, God's spiritual Israel, that is composed of Gentiles who previously were not counted as God's people as well as believing Jews. Peter's audience then, is anyone who is "In Christ". We have to conclude then that all born-again believers are called to be priests to our God. The first order of business then, it would seem to me, would be to determine what a priest is and what his duties are or were.

We get our first glimpse of this term in Genesis 14:18 "Then Melchizedek king of Salem brought out bread and wine; he was the priest of God Most High". The story revolves around the account of Abraham. Abraham and Lot, you might recall had come into the land of Canaan while over time they both became wealthy eventually having to separate from one another. Lot chose a fertile land and became involved in a local dispute where war broke out with Lot and his entire family along with all his possessions were taken captive. Abraham heard about it and came to the rescue and defeated the people who had taken Lot captive and took all the spoils of war. On the way back home from this war he met Melchizedek and gave him a tithe of all he had taken. Note two very important details that show something of what a function of a Priest is:

1. Abraham gave him an offering of his possessions and Melchizedek took them,
2. Melchizedek in turn blessed Abraham which blessing God honored.

> Genesis 14: 19–20 "Blessed be Abram of God Most High, Possessor of heaven and earth. And blessed be God Most High, Who has delivered your enemies into your hand"

And of course, the New Testament book of Hebrews reveals that this Melchizedek was a foreshadowing of the Priesthood of Christ and in turn our Priesthood as Christ's body. (see Hebrews 7: all, but especially vv. 1–3 & 17–22)

We would need to read most of the first five books of the Bible, known as the Pentateuch, to really understand what a priest's duties were and what the sacrifices were that they offered on a daily basis, but the New Testament book of Hebrews does a great job of explaining it in much fewer words, so let's turn there to get an understanding of exactly what a priest's duties were and what the nature of the sacrifices were that they offered.

The writer of Hebrews again gives us the answer; "5 For every high priest taken from among men is appointed for men in things pertaining to God, that he may offer both gifts and sacrifices for sins" (Hebrews 5:1-2). We can see clearly that a priest was a person chosen by God to, 1) represent other people in their dealings with God, and 2) to make atonement for the sins the people had committed so the people would not lose their standing before God by offering blood sacrifices. Consequently, we have to conclude that God's heart was that the nation of Israel was to be a kingdom of priests and a holy nation that would be a light set on a hill showing forth the praises of their God (Exodus 19:6).

However, because Israel failed so miserably in fulfilling this mission, God called and anointed another Priest that would fulfill that mission "according to the order of Melchizedek" (Hebrews 5:6). Now, even the writer confesses that some of the details concerning this Old Testament Priest that only shows up one time, is ". . . hard to explain, since you have become dull of hearing" (Hebrews 5:11). But, nevertheless, he goes on to explain, that because there was a change in the priesthood, there must "of necessity there is also a change of the law" (Hebrews 7:12). Further, the writer of Hebrews goes on to explain in some detail the provisions of that "new law".

> For every high priest is appointed to offer both gifts and sacrifices. Therefore, it is necessary that this One also have something to offer. For if He were on earth, He would not be a priest, since there are priests who offer the gifts according to the law; who serve the copy and shadow of the heavenly things, as Moses was divinely instructed when he was about to make the tabernacle. For He said, "See that you make all things according to the pattern shown you on the mountain." But now He has obtained a more excellent ministry, inasmuch as He is also Mediator of a better covenant, which was established on better promises. (Hebrews 8:1–6)

And then adds one further important point concerning Christ as this new Priest establishing the new covenant.

> And every priest stands ministering daily and offering repeatedly the same sacrifices, which can never take away sins. But this Man, after He had offered one sacrifice for sins forever, sat down at the right hand of God, from that time waiting till His enemies are made His footstool. For by one offering He has perfected forever those who are being sanctified. But the Holy Spirit also witnesses to us; for after He had said before, "This is the covenant that I will make with them after those days, says the Lord: I will put My laws into their hearts, and in their minds I will write them," then He adds, "Their sins and their lawless deeds I will remember no more." Now where there is remission of these, there is no longer an offering for sin. (Hebrews 10:11–18).

Let us pause and briefly summarize what we have established up to this point before we can proceed with the application of this important point. First, all born-again Christians are called and set apart as a Royal Priesthood. In other words, if you are a born-again Christian, you are an ordained Priest and therefore, responsible before God to carry out the duties of a Priest. And second, we do not offer sacrifices to God for the sins or ourselves and the people as the old priesthood did. Why, you might ask? Because Jesus did that once and for all time (Hebrews 10:10). Third is the all-important question of what exactly are we to sacrifice as New Covenant Priests since we no longer need to offer the blood sacrifices specified in the law of Moses? And, of course, foundational to this question is an understanding of exactly what is the meaning of "sacrifice"? I believe rather than trying to give some dictionary or academic definition of sacrifice, it might be much clearer to look at a biblical example. The setting is a story of David who had come under the judgment of God. David had committed a grievous sin in the sight of God by numbering the people of Israel for his own glory rather than at God's command. Therefore, the judgment of God was upon him. Consequently, he determined, as was his custom, to seek God's forgiveness and grace by offering a sacrifice as demanded by the law.

> So David, according to the word of Gad, went up as the Lord commanded. Now Araunah looked, and saw the king and his servants coming toward him. So Araunah went out and bowed before the king with his face to the ground.
>
> Then Araunah said, "Why has my lord the king come to his servant?"
>
> And David said, "To buy the threshing floor from you, to build an altar to the Lord, that the plague may be withdrawn from the people."

Now Araunah said to David, "Let my lord the king take and offer up whatever seems good to him. Look, here are oxen for burnt sacrifice, and threshing implements and the yokes of the oxen for wood. All these, O king, Araunah has given to the king."

And Araunah said to the king, "May the Lord your God accept you."

Then the king said to Araunah, "No, but I will surely buy it from you for a price; nor will I offer burnt offerings to the Lord my God with that which costs me nothing." So David bought the threshing floor and the oxen for fifty shekels of silver. And David built there an altar to the Lord, and offered burnt offerings and peace offerings. So the Lord heeded the prayers for the land, and the plague was withdrawn from Israel. (2 Samuel 24:19–25)

Carefully notice David's response to Arunah when he offered to just give him the land, David said "nor will I offer burnt offerings to the Lord my God with that which costs me nothing." In other words, David understood clearly that it is not a sacrifice if it does not cost the giver something. So, we must conclude that a sacrifice that is acceptable to the Lord is something that costs you something. It if is just excess, blemished, or second class, it is NOT a sacrifice. Listen to the prophet Malachi's teaching on this subject to see God's heart concerning sacrifice.

A son honors his father,
And a servant his master.
If then I am the Father,
Where is My honor?
And if I am a Master,
Where is My reverence?
Says the Lord of hosts
To you priests who despise My name.

Yet you say, 'In what way have we despised Your name?'
You offer defiled food on My altar,
But say,'In what way have we defiled You?'
By saying, 'The table of the Lord is contemptible.'
And when you offer the blind as a sacrifice,
Is it not evil?
And when you offer the lame and sick,
Is it not evil?
Offer it then to your governor!
Would he be pleased with you?
Would he accept you favorably?"
Says the Lord of hosts.
But now entreat God's favor,
That He may be gracious to us.
While this is being done by your hands,
Will He accept you favorably?"
Says the Lord of hosts.
Who is there even among you who would shut the doors,
So that you would not kindle fire on My altar in vain?
I have no pleasure in you,
"Says the Lord of hosts,"
Nor will I accept an offering from your hands.
For from the rising of the sun, even to its going down,
My name shall be great among the Gentiles;
In every place incense shall be offered to My name,
And a pure offering;
For My name shall be great among the nations,"
Says the Lord of hosts. (Malachi 1:6–11)

So, it becomes obvious that God expects a sacrifice to actually cost us something, to be something valuable to us and acceptable to Him. We need to understand as well that in the Old Testament, Gentiles were anyone not a member of the Nation of Israel. But in the New Testament, a Gentile is anyone who is not born-again of the Spirit of God, or an unbeliever.

Before we undertake finding the New Testament sacrifices, we need to pause briefly and summarize what we have learned so far. First, of course, is the simple fact that all born again Christians, the church, have been called and appointed as priests to our God. Second, we are called to minister for the Gentiles (the world of unbelievers). And third, the sacrifices we offer are not for our benefit alone but as a witness to unbelievers in our effort to bring others to a saving knowledge of Jesus. As a side note: signs and wonders and gifts of the Spirit are not for our own benefit alone or to make us look or feel good, but to bring attention to the Glory of God and bring others to Jesus.

I am reminded of a story I heard years ago about a small country church whose pastor passed away and the elder board began the task of finding a new pastor for their congregation. After a long search, they finally received an application from a young man who had a national reputation of being a great preacher. So they invited him to the church to try out. They were impressed so they hired him as their new pastor. The whole community was excited and showed up for the first Sunday service. This young man preached his first sermon and the people were very impressed and heaped praise on him on what a good job he had done. The next week even more people show up for the Sunday service and the pastor gets up and preaches the exact same sermon he had preached on the first Sunday. Everyone enjoyed it and still heaped praise on him for such a good sermon, assuming he had preached the same sermon because of so many new people. The third Sunday comes along and many people show up excited to hear him preach. But the pastor gets up and preaches the exact sermon for the third time. This time only a few offers him praise for his sermon and the elders begin to talk among themselves wondering if there is something wrong with him that he only knows one sermon. But they still hold onto hope and the fourth Sunday comes and sure enough, the pastor gets up and preaches the exact same sermon again. This time the elders decide to confront him and find out why he keeps preaching the same sermon. So, they go to him and ask why, and his response takes them back. He simply said, "Well, when you start living the first sermon, then I will move on to another!"

We are responsible for how we hear and what we do with what we hear (see Mark 4:23-25). The Word of God is not some theory to accept but a lifestyle to be lived. God will hold us accountable for what we know so listen and follow the example of the church in Berea who searched the Scriptures diligently to see if what Paul was teaching to them was correct according to the Scriptures (see Acts 17: 10ff). The fact of the matter is God called you, saved you, gifted you and now He expects you to be the Christian He has made you.

Let's examine the Word of God to see what these spiritual sacrifices are that we as Priests of the Most High God are commanded to offer. I have identified seven, however, there might be more. I don't claim this as an exhaustive list, but a suggestive list. The point is that we as priests of God Most High, need to be about our assigned duties.

The first is our bodies. Listen to Paul explain.

> I beseech you therefore, brethren, by the mercies of God, that you present your bodies a living sacrifice, holy, acceptable to God, which is your reasonable service. And do not be conformed to this world, but be transformed by the renewing of your mind, that you may prove what is that good and acceptable and perfect will of God. (Romans 12:1–2)

Jesus first revealed to us the true intent for our bodies when He declared that the people would tear the temple down and He would rebuild it in three days. And of course, just as we do, the Jews misunderstood what Jesus said; "Then the Jews said, 'It has taken forty-six years to build this temple, and will You raise it up in three days?' But He was speaking of the temple of His body" (John 2:20–21).

Jesus reveals to us that the post-Levitical Priesthood would minister in the new temple – our bodies and in reality the Body of Christ – the Church. This is an important foundational truth that we must understand if we are going to fulfill God's purpose for our lives. We are individually temples of the Holy Spirit when we are born-again of the Spirit. However, God never intended for us to be an island unto ourselves. Rather, just like a body has many parts and each part must fulfill its proper function, so we must be part of the larger body of believers each fulfilling our specific function in order to be a whole healthy functioning body. Or as Jesus said, "I am the vine, you are the branches. He who abides in Me, and I in him, bears much fruit; for without Me you can do nothing" (John 15:5). And it wasn't just Jesus's body that was a temple, it is ours as well when we are born-again.

> Or do you not know that your body is the temple of the Holy Spirit who is in you, whom you have from God, and you are not your own? For you were bought at a price; therefore glorify God in your body and in your spirit, which are God's (1 Corinthians 6:19–20)

Because our bodies are a temple of the Holy Spirit, we are given several admonitions concerning our bodies and how we should keep them. Remember that according to the Law not only the priest had to be purified by wearing his priestly garments and by washing himself before entering the tabernacle, but the animal that was being sacrificed had to be without any blemish. Therefore, it is not surprising that God would give directives on how we should present ourselves to Him. Listen to these instructions:

1. Romans 6:12 "Therefore do not let sin reign in your mortal body, that you should obey it in its lusts."
2. Romans 8:13–14 "For if you live according to the flesh you will die; but if by the Spirit you put to death the deeds of the body, you will live."
   - This would include things such as sexual sin, excessive drinking, drugs, gluttony, or anything that is harmful to your body.
3. 1 Corinthians 9:27 "But I discipline my body and bring it into subjection, lest, when I have preached to others, I myself should become disqualified."

Or how about our "Spiritual Body"? Is it possible that we can defile that as well? The Apostle Paul claims that we have every bit as much responsibility (maybe even more) to take care of Christ's Body – His Church, as we do of taking care of our own physical body. Pay attention to what Paul teaches us in his letter to the Corinthian church. He is instructing the church at Corinth concerning partaking of the "Lord's Supper" or as we call it today, communion. The church had been practicing it in a wrong, selfish manner and Paul was clear that they were under the Lord's judgment because of it.

> Therefore whoever eats this bread or drinks this cup of the Lord in an unworthy manner will be guilty of the body and blood of the Lord. But let a man examine himself, and so let him eat of the bread and drink of the cup. For he who eats and drinks in an unworthy manner eats and drinks judgment to himself, not discerning the Lord's body. For this reason many are weak and sick among you, and many sleep. For if we would judge ourselves, we would not be judged. But when we are judged, we are chastened by the Lord, that we may not be condemned with the world. (1 Corinthians 11:27–32)

Every believer needs to understand clearly what God holds us accountable for. God has saved us and baptized us in the very same Spirit that raised Jesus from the dead and He now dwells in us and we need to acknowledge that allowing the Spirit to lead us into the ministry that He has ordained for us and that involves sacrificing our own right to our own body and allowing Him to incorporate it into His spiritual body, His church to use as He sees fit not as we do. This He calls sacrificing our bodies for His glory. Let us move on to the second spiritual sacrifice we are commanded to offer.

Number two is a very fascinating command where the Apostle Paul shows us that we are to offer up as a sacrifice to God people won for Christ.

> Nevertheless, brethren, I have written more boldly to you on some points, as reminding you, because of the grace

given to me by God, that I might be a minister of Jesus Christ to the Gentiles, ministering the gospel of God, that the offering of the Gentiles might be acceptable, sanctified by the Holy Spirit. (Romans 15:15–16)

In this case I like the New American Bible Translation of this verse because it makes it extremely clear Paul's intent.

(I have been appointed) to be a minister of Christ Jesus to the Gentiles in performing the priestly service of the gospel of God, so that the offering up of the Gentiles may be acceptable, sanctified by the Holy Spirit. In Christ Jesus, then, I have reason to boast in what pertains to God. (Romans 15:16 –17 NAB)[22]

His point is clear, he offered as a sacrifice to God those people he had labored endlessly for and won to Christ. You and I as members of Christ's body and His acting priests need to ask ourselves some very hard questions to see if we are offering sacrifices acceptable to God.

1. Do we labor in the Harvest fields that are "white unto harvest" to bring as many people as possible to Christ? Do we labor/sacrifice time, effort, and sometimes even money to "(B)e diligent to present yourself approved to God, a worker who does not need to be ashamed, rightly dividing the word of truth. (2 Timothy 2:15)?

2. Are we prepared to ". . . in your hearts set apart Christ as Lord. Always be prepared to give an answer to everyone who asks you to give the reason for the hope that you have. But do this with gentleness and respect," (1 Peter 3:15)?

Even if we are not a preacher or teacher, we are ALL called to share

---

[22] The **New American Bible** (**NAB**) is an English translation of the Bible first published in 1970. The 1986 Revised NAB is the basis of the revised Lectionary, and it is the only translation approved for use at Mass in the Catholic dioceses of the United States and the Philippines, and the 1970 first edition is also an approved Bible translation by the Episcopal Church in the United States.

our faith. Those we lead to Christ are not for our glory. They are not to be put on a badge to bring attention or glory to ourselves. How many preachers and evangelists focus on numbers for their efforts and advertise as "the fruit of MY labor"? We are called to give God the glory and Him alone.

Now we move on the third spiritual sacrifice we as priests of God Most High are called to offer. And this is probably the hardest for most people because it involves one of our favorite idols, money.

> Now you Philippians know also that in the beginning of the gospel, when I departed from Macedonia, no church shared with me concerning giving and receiving but you only. For even in Thessalonica you sent aid once and again for my necessities. Not that I seek the gift, but I seek the fruit that abounds to your account. Indeed I have all and abound. I am full, having received from Epaphroditus the things sent from you, a sweet-smelling aroma, an acceptable sacrifice, well pleasing to God. And my God shall supply all your need according to His riches in glory by Christ Jesus. Now to our God and Father be glory forever and ever. Amen (Philippians 4:15–20).

Of course, we always like to quote v. 19 "And my God shall supply all your need according to His riches in glory by Christ Jesus." However, it must be understood in the context in which it was written. We must always remember that we have to read and interpret Scripture in the context in which it was written. Paul spent the first part of his letter commending the Philippian church on their generosity and faithfulness in giving. Consequently, we have to understand that Paul is teaching that it is ONLY as we give first that God can produce the "crop" to supply all our needs. The farmer does not reap a crop until the seed is first planted. And as with a lot of seeds we sow, it sometimes can take years to get the first fruit and for many years to come you must tend the orchard in order for it to continue to produce a good fruitful crop. That is, it must be pruned, watered, and the fruit must be harvested.

Remember here as well the first thing David taught us about a sacrifice. It is not a real sacrifice unless it costs you something. So here he is not suggesting that you only give out of your great abundance, but that giving becomes a lifestyle and sacrificially means that you give out of your necessity, not only out of your abundance. Although it is not a popular teaching for many Christian's in the 21ˢᵗ century, the tithe is still a biblical practice that needs to be understood and practiced. Many people assume that tithing is an Old Testament concept that was part of the Law of Moses that was fulfilled with Christ, so tithing is no longer valid for today. However, this is a lie from the very pit of hell. The tithe was instituted many centuries before Moses and the Law when Abraham paid a tithe to Melchizedek. While we do not have a record of God teaching Moses, or Melchizedek the practice, it is evident that they both were very familiar with the practice, and later God simple wrote it into the law, but it was not unique with the law. The Prophet Malachi also spoke rather pointedly concerning the tithe and elaborated some on the purpose of the tithe. Pay close attention to his words and we will learn something of God's purpose in the tithe. But first we must remember that one of the first principles that God instituted at creation was the principal that every seed would reproduce after its own kind.

> Then God said, "Let the earth bring forth grass, the herb that yields seed, and the fruit tree that yields fruit according to its kind, whose seed is in itself, on the earth"; and it was so. And the earth brought forth grass, the herb that yields seed according to its kind, and the tree that yields fruit, whose seed is in itself according to its kind. And God saw that it was good. So the evening and the morning were the third day (Genesis 1:11–13).

Therefore. listen to what Malachi said concerning the tithe.

> Will a man rob God?
> Yet you have robbed Me!
> But you say,'

> In what way have we robbed You?
> 'In tithes and offerings.
> You are cursed with a curse,
> For you have robbed Me,
> Even this whole nation.
> Bring all the tithes into the storehouse,
> That there may be food in My house,
> And try Me now in this,
> "Says the Lord of hosts,
> "If I will not open for you the windows of heaven
> And pour out for you such blessing
> That there will not be room enough to receive it.
> And I will rebuke the devourer for your sakes,
> So that he will not destroy the fruit of your ground,
> Nor shall the vine fail to bear fruit for you in the field,"
> Says the Lord of hosts;
> And all nations will call you blessed,
> For you will be a delightful land,"
> Says the Lord of hosts. (Malachi 3:8–12)

Listen dear reader, tithing is not a burden or some legalistic law that one must practice or risk coming under the judgment of God. It is God's generous provision for us to have every need met. While God did fulfill the Law of Moses and release us from its burdensome regulations, He did not do away with His laws of creation that always have and always will be a part of God's plan and provision for our well-being. Try jumping off a tall building and ignoring the law of gravity! You will still find that it is a valid law that we must know and respect lest we pay a steep price for ignoring it. God never eliminated the law of sowing and reaping. Try going out to your field and reaping a harvest without first planting a crop of good seed! In the same way, how can we expect to have our every need met financially without first planting the seed? Then and only then can we reasonably expect to reap a crop. This is why Paul told the Corinthians to give generously. "But as you abound in everything — in faith, in speech, in knowledge, in all diligence, and in your love for us

— see that you abound in this grace also" (2 Corinthians 8:7). Of course, when you read the verse in its context, you will find that he is talking about their generous giving and their support of his ministry. So, giving is God's way of taking care of our every need, and the sooner we realize that the sooner we will understand the value of this sacrifice. You won't just give out of your abundance, but you will joyfully give out of your need, knowing that you cannot outgive God.

Also remember that some seeds take much longer to produce fruit, so we need to learn to wait patiently for our seed to mature. However, as David teaches us in Psalm, we can test in the fact that we will reap:

> Rest in the Lord, and wait patiently for Him;
> Do not fret because of him who prospers in his way,
> Because of the man who brings wicked schemes to pass.
> Cease from anger, and forsake wrath;
> Do not fret — it only causes harm. (Psalm 37:7–8)

And now we move on to the fourth sacrifice that the New Testament Priesthood is called to offer, and that is praise and worship. This one I believe is one of the most misunderstood elements of modern worship. We continually refer to the "singing" portion of our services as the "worship service". However, this is not the biblical concept of worship. Indeed, it is one element, but only one element, and taken separately can actually lead one away from true worship. I hope to leave you with the understanding that biblical worship acceptable to God is a pure, holy lifestyle not just on Sunday morning, but seven days a week before the non-believers. "Therefore by Him let us continually offer the sacrifice of praise to God, that is, the fruit of our lips, giving thanks to His name" (Hebrews 13:15).

Listen for a moment to what the Bible says concerning our worship of God –

Exodus 20:7 "You shall not take the name of the Lord your God in vain, for the Lord will not hold him guiltless who takes His name in vain. The word for "vain" from the Nelson's New Illustrated Bible Dictionary means:

> **VANITY** — emptiness, worthlessness, or futility. The word occurs about 37 times in the Old Testament (NKJV), most frequently in Ecclesiastes. The word "vanity" as used in the Bible does not mean conceit or a "superiority complex," like the modern meaning of the term. When applied to persons, it means emptiness or futility of natural human life (Job 7:3; Eccl. 1:2; 2:1; 4:4; 1:10).

When applied to things, vanity is especially used to describe idols, because there is no spiritual reality to them (Isaiah 41:29). Believers are urged to stay away from vain things and to live their lives in the understanding that they are engaged in a growing relationship with Christ. Anything short of God Himself that people trust to meet their deepest needs is vanity (Ephesians 4:17–24).

Besides admonishing the people to be ready to give a defense of their faith to anyone who might ask, Peter says:[23]

1 Peter 3:16 "But do this in a gentle and respectful way. Keep your conscience clear. Then if people speak against you, they will be ashamed when they see what a good life you live because you belong to Christ." The fact of the matter is that if you genuinely love Jesus, you can't hide it. There is no such thing as a "secret" love for Christ. Just like Isaac who had lied to the king by telling him that Rebecca was his sister, but as the king watched their interaction through a window and saw Isaac showing affection to her and knew that she was in fact his wife, so in the same way, if you truly love Jesus, you can't hide it.

> Now it came to pass, when he had been there a long time, that Abimelech king of the Philistines looked through a window, and saw, and there was Isaac, showing endearment to Rebekah his wife. Then Abimelech called Isaac and said, "Quite obviously she is your wife; so how could you say, 'She is my sister'?" (Genesis 26:8–9).

---

[23] definition for vanity taken from Prayer - Easton's Bible Dictionary Online (biblestudytools.com)

Remember what Peter taught us about our role in the world. "But you are a chosen generation, a royal priesthood, a holy nation, His own special people, that you may **proclaim the praises** of Him who called you out of darkness into His marvelous light;" (1 Peter 2:9). Spiritual Praise is a lifestyle that brings glory to the Name of the LORD. God takes our portrayal of ourselves as Christians to the world very seriously. True praise to God is to proclaim the Good news of the Gospel with our lives, with our words, with our actions, and when we do that, it will manifest itself in our lives as the fruit of the Spirit ". . . love, joy, peace, longsuffering, kindness, goodness, faithfulness, gentleness, self-control" (Galatians 5:22–23).

The fruits of a life of praise and worship to God are many and I have taken most of these examples from Revelation where we get a glimpse of true praise around the throne of God because we are commanded to worship God in spirit and truth (John 4:24). I as well have chosen some examples from the Psalms where David has much to teach us about worship. I felt this might be the most accurate glimpse into what is entailed in true worship in spirit and in truth. This is not meant to be an exhaustive list of praise and worship, but my prayer is that it will instill a hunger in the reader so that you will do a more exhaustive search of Scripture becoming a worshipper that truly brings glory and honor to our Savior Jesus Christ.

1. **Singing** – Revelation 5:9–10
    And they sang a new song, saying:
    "You are worthy to take the scroll,
    And to open its seals;
    For You were slain,
    And have redeemed us to God by Your blood
    Out of every tribe and tongue and people and nation,
    And have made us kings and priests to our God;
    And we shall reign on the earth."

2. **Loud Praises** – Revelation 5:12
   Saying with a loud voice:
   "Worthy is the Lamb who was slain
   To receive power and riches and wisdom,
   And strength and honor and glory and blessing!"

3. **Prayers** – Hebrews 5:7 "who, in the days of His flesh, when He had offered up prayers and supplications, with vehement cries and tears to Him who was able to save Him from death, and was heard because of His godly fear,"

4. **Thanksgiving** – Revelation 4:9–11 & 7:12

   Whenever the living creatures give glory and honor and thanks to Him who sits on the throne, who lives forever and ever, the twenty-four elders fall down before Him who sits on the throne and worship Him who lives forever and ever, and cast their crowns before the throne, saying:

   > You are worthy, O Lord,
   > To receive glory and honor and power;
   > For You created all things,
   > And by Your will they exist and were created."
   > And Revelation 7:12
   > saying: "Amen! Blessing and glory and wisdom,
   > Thanksgiving and honor and power and might,
   > Be to our God forever and ever. Amen."

5. **Dancing** – 2 Samuel 6:16 (David) "Now as the ark of the Lord came into the City of David, Michal, Saul's daughter, looked through a window and saw King David leaping and whirling before the Lord; and she despised him in her heart.

   and

Psalm 30: 11–12

You have turned for me my mourning into dancing;

You have put off my sackcloth and clothed me with gladness,

To the end that my glory may sing praise to You and not be silent.

O Lord my God, I will give thanks to You forever.

6. **<u>Skillfully playing instruments</u>** – Psalm 33:3 "Sing to Him a new song; Play skillfully with a shout of joy."

And a complete search of Scripture might reveal even more specifics, but the point is, that true worship in Spirit and Truth is a complete lifestyle that brings glory to God that produces the fruit of the Spirit and all of their accompanying manifestations.

So far we have discussed four spiritual sacrifices, so let's move on to another. The fifth spiritual sacrifice we as Priests of God Most High are called to offer are our good works. This one is a bit harder to define, but I believe that it is worth investigating so we can offer it to God as a faithful Priest unto our God. I will begin by giving a Bible Dictionary definition of the term "good works".

Works are "good" only when, (1) they spring from the principle of love to God. The moral character of an act is determined by the moral principle that prompts it. Faith and love in the heart are the essential elements of all true obedience. Hence good works only spring from a believing heart, can only be wrought by one reconciled to God (Ephesians 2:10 ; James 2:18:22).

Good works have the glory of God as their object; and (3) they have the revealed will of God as their only rule (Deuteronomy 12:32 ; Revelation 22:18 Revelation 22:19).

Good works are an expression of gratitude in the believer's heart (John 14:15 John 14:23 ; Galatians 5:6). They are the fruits of the Spirit (Titus 2:10-12), and thus spring from grace, which they illustrate and strengthen in the heart.

Good works of the most sincere believers are all imperfect, yet like their persons they are accepted through the mediation of Jesus Christ (Colossians 3:17), and so are rewarded; they have no merit intrinsically, but are rewarded wholly of grace.[24]

We see the principle of good works being an acceptable sacrifice in Hebrews 13:16 "But do not forget to do good and to share, for with such sacrifices God is well pleased." Doing good works is a recognized spiritual sacrifice before God as well. James too speaks of the importance of doing good works.

But be doers of the word, and not hearers only, deceiving yourselves. For if anyone is a hearer of the word and not a doer, he is like a man observing his natural face in a mirror; for he observes himself, goes away, and immediately forgets what kind of man he was. But he who looks into the perfect law of liberty and continues in it and is not a forgetful hearer but a doer of the work, this one will be blessed in what he does. (James 1:22–25).

Now the fruit (works) of the Spirit are described in Galatians 5 this way:

Now the works of the flesh are evident, which are: adultery, fornication, uncleanness, lewdness, idolatry,

[24] M.G. Easton M.A., D.D., Illustrated Bible Dictionary, Third Edition, published by Thomas Nelson, 1897. Public Domain,

sorcery, hatred, contentions, jealousies, outbursts of wrath, selfish ambitions, dissensions, heresies, envy, murders, drunkenness, revelries, and the like; of which I tell you beforehand, just as I also told you in time past, that those who practice such things will not inherit the kingdom of God.

But the fruit of the Spirit is love, joy, peace, longsuffering, kindness, goodness, faithfulness, gentleness, self-control. Against such there is no law. And those who are Christ's have crucified the flesh with its passions and desires. If we live in the Spirit, let us also walk in the Spirit. Let us not become conceited, provoking one another, envying one another. (Galatians 5:19–26)

And John 9:4 teaches us another important principle when it comes to work: "Jesus declared, "I must work the works of Him who sent Me while it is day; the night is coming when no one can work". Basically, the point is that whatever your hand finds to do, do it with all of your might as unto the Lord and not for the recognition (Ecclesiastes 9:10).

I know that a lot more could be said about being engaged in good works, but I pray the reader realizes that anything you do for "the least of these" (Matthew 25:40 & 45) is considered good by God, so let me just conclude this section with the encouragement to actively be aware of your surroundings and the Lord will lead you into your good work that He wants you to be engaged in.

Now we will move on to the sixth acceptable sacrifice that the Priest of God Most High will offer to God. And that is a broken heart. Listen to the Psalmist as he declares God's heart.

The sacrifices of God are a broken spirit,
A broken and a contrite heart —
These, O God, You will not despise (Psalm 51:17).

And Jesus agreed as He taught an important lesson for us in the Beatitudes as recorded by Matthew. "Blessed are the meek, for they shall inherit the earth" (Matthew 5:5). Because meek is a term we don't hear much in the 21ˢᵗ Century, so let's go to a Bible Dictionary again to get a biblical definition.

> **MEEKNESS** — an attitude of humility toward God and gentleness toward people, springing from a recognition that God is in control. Although weakness and meekness may look similar, they are not the same. Weakness is due to negative circumstances, such as lack of strength or lack of courage. But meekness is due to a person's conscious choice. It is strength and courage under control, coupled with kindness.
>
> The apostle Paul once pointed out that the spiritual leaders of the church have great power, even leverage, in confronting a sinner. But he cautioned them to retrain themselves in meekness (Gal. 6:1; 5:22–23). As such it is part of the equipment that every follower of Jesus should wear (2 Cor. 10:1; Gal. 5:23; 6:1; Eph. 4:1–2).[25]

Also, a broken heart for the lost is part of having God's heart. God so loved the world, and especially the people in it, that He gave up His very own Son so we could be saved (John 3:16). God intends that His Royal Priesthood will share His heart and do the same. After all, Jesus did charge His disciples at the last supper before His crucifixion, with a new commandment to do so.

> A new commandment I give to you, that you love one another; as I have loved you, that you also love one another. By this all will know that you are My disciples, if you have love for one another" (John 13:34–35).

---

[25] Nelson's Illustrated Bible Dictionary, Edited by Ronald F. Youngblood, ©1995, 1986, Thomas Nelson Publishers, p. 817

So, the charge is to offer to God a humble, broken heart and let Him give you His heart which is entirely focused on a lost and dying world. A heart that does not seek its own pleasure and well-being, but is focused on fulfilling the Great Commission given by Jesus to:

> Go therefore and make disciples of all the nations, baptizing them in the name of the Father and of the Son and of the Holy Spirit, teaching them to observe all things that I have commanded you; and lo, I am with you always, even to the end of the age (Matthew 28:19–20).

I want to move on to the seventh and last sacrifice the Royal Priest of God Most High is called to offer, which is believing Prayer. I'm sure that an accomplished Bible student could identify more, but I believe this list will be a good place for most believers to begin. So, let's begin by looking at what Scripture says concerning prayer. I will reference a Bible Dictionary one more time to get a biblical definition of prayer. Most people have heard the term and most people admit to praying at times. However, prayer is an activity that is so important to the Christian walk, that I don't want to leave anything to chance, especially on what the Bible means when it mentions prayer.

> Prayer is conversing with God; the intercourse of the soul with God, not in contemplation or meditation, but in direct address to him. Prayer may be oral or mental, occasional or constant, ejaculatory or formal. It is a "beseeching the Lord" (Exodus 32:11); "pouring out the soul before the Lord" (1 Samuel 1:15); "praying and crying to heaven" (2 Chronicles 32:20); "seeking unto God and making supplication" (Job 8:5); "drawing near to God" (Psalms 73:28); "bowing the knees" (Ephesians 3:14).

> Prayer presupposes a belief in the personality of God, His ability and willingness to hold intercourse with us, His

personal control of all things and of all His creatures and all their actions.

Acceptable prayer must be sincere (Hebrews 10:22), offered with reverence and godly fear, with a humble sense of our own insignificance as creatures and of our own unworthiness as sinners, with earnest importunity, and with unhesitating submission to the divine will. Prayer must also be offered in the faith that God is, and is the hearer and answerer of prayer, and that He will fulfil his word, "Ask, and you shall receive" (Matthew 7:7 Matthew 7:8 ; 21:22 ; Mark 11:24 ; John 14:13 John 14:14), and in the name of Christ (John 16:23 John 16:24 ; 15:16 ; Ephesians 2:18 ; 5:20 ; Colossians 3:17 ; 1 Peter 2:5).[26]

David was a man of pray and he believed in the power of prayer. Mainly because he experienced the Lord answering his prayers throughout his entire lifetime. And we can learn much from him concerning prayer.

Lord, I cry out to You;
Make haste to me!
Give ear to my voice when I cry out to You.
Let my prayer be set before You as incense,
The lifting up of my hands as the evening sacrifice
(Psalm 141:1–2).

And, of course, Revelation 5:8 reveals that "incense" is the prayers of the saints. There is really no specific form for prayer laid out anywhere in Scripture. There is mention made of kneeling in prayer; of bowing and falling prostrate; of spreading out the hands and of standing. Even the Lord's prayer that He gave when the disciples asked Him to teach them to pray, was not a formula, but an outline and model of prayer, not a prayer to memorize and repeat back to Him. So, one must conclude that there is no

---

[26] Illustrated Bible Dictionary, M.G. Easton Public Domain (definition taken from Prayer - Easton's Bible Dictionary Online (biblestudytools.com)

right way to pray, but that we should be engaged in it at all times as Paul instructed in his letter to the Thessalonians, to "pray without ceasing" (1 Thessalonians 5:17).

There are different types of prayer mentioned in the Scriptures, but no prescribed Scriptures. Again, this is not meant to be an exhaustive list, but a suggestive list that are plainly outlined with examples.

1. Public prayer (Isiah 56:7),
2. Corporate Prayer (Matthew 12:21),
3. Intercessory Prayer (Romans 8:26),
4. Petitionary Prayer (specific) (Philippians 4:6), and
5. Closet Prayer (Matthew6:6)

I challenge the reader to investigate some of these topics further and begin to really engage the Lord in prayer. It is the manner in which, when coupled with serious Bible study, you will engage the God of the universe and you will quickly discover that He not only answers and responds to prayer, but He can move mountains and change circumstances in your life. Don't ever forget that a priest's purpose is to represent God to a lost and dying world and we can approach Him boldly as His priest.

So the question needs to be asked now that we have identified the spiritual sacrifices that the Priests of God are called on to offer, how do we apply it in a practical day-to-day basis in our lives?

1. Our bodies
2. People Won for Christ
3. Sacrificial Giving
4. Praise & Worship
5. Good Works
6. A Broken Heart
7. Believing Prayer

Listen carefully to what the writer of Hebrews teaches us about our new priesthood. "We have an altar from which those who serve the (earthly) tabernacle have no right to eat" (Hebrews 13:10). We need to understand clearly that the altar is Jesus and all we are, all we have, and all we do are to be through Him and for Him. That is a very real spiritual sacrifice. And the fruit of those sacrifices are precious and many. Listen to the Apostle Paul describe the fruit he realized as a faithful priest of God Most High.

Do we begin again to commend ourselves? Or do we need, as some others, epistles of commendation to you or letters of commendation from you? You are our epistle written in our hearts, known and read by all men; clearly you are an epistle of Christ, ministered by us, written not with ink but by the Spirit of the living God, not on tablets of stone but on tablets of flesh, that is, of the heart (2 Corinthians 3:1–3).

The above is an example of how a faithful people in real life go about performing their task as a priest of God Most High. Paul was depending on the church in Corinth to support his missionary efforts and he was very pleasantly surprised by their generosity and willingness to sacrifice, not just for his sake, but for the Lord's sake as His priest. Listen to his response to their faithfulness:

> For I bear witness that according to their ability, yes, and beyond their ability, they were freely willing, imploring us with much urgency that we would receive the gift and the fellowship of the ministering to the saints. And not only as we had hoped, but they first gave themselves to the Lord, and then to us by the will of God (2 Corinthians 8:3–5).

Before we can bring our <u>material gifts</u> to the LORD we must first bring/give ourselves.

Before we can bring our <u>spiritual gifts</u> to the LORD we must first bring/give ourselves.

Before we can hope to produce the Fruit of the Spirit, we must first be filled and controlled by the Holy Spirit.

In short, Jesus must truly be LORD of our life, not just in a hypothetical way, but in a very real day-to-day, decision-by decision way, manifesting Himself in and through you.

I want to complete this chapter on what it means to be a Christian by reminding you of who you are and encourage you to enter into your position in the body of Christ, His church as a full and active participant:

> But you are a chosen generation, a royal priesthood, a holy nation, His own special people, that you may proclaim the praises of Him who called you out of darkness into His marvelous light; who once were not a people but are now the people of God, who had not obtained mercy but now have obtained mercy" (1 Peter 2:9–10).

Did you notice the purpose God determined for making you His priest? Peter indicates that the purpose is so "that you may proclaim the praises of Him who called you out of darkness into His marvelous light."

Are you up to the challenge? Simply say yes LORD and watch Him work it out in your life. Not in a day, not in a week, and not even in a year, but He will work, and you will be changed as you submit to His leadership and offer Him the prescribed sacrifices He has commissioned you to offer as His Royal Holy Priest.

As I close out this discussion, let me encourage you to remember what coach Mike McDonald said, "Success isn't built in a day, but it's built daily!"[27]

---

[27] Success Isn't Built in a Day, It's Built Daily (coachmikemacdonald.com) https://coachmikemacdonald.com/success-isnt-built-in-a-day-its-built-daily/ accessed 4/9/2021